Supernatural Miracles and Visions Stories

Shekinah Glory

Frances Purnell Dampier

Shekinah Glory: Supernatural Miracles and Visions Stories
Copyright © 2023 by Frances Purnell Dampier

Published in the United States of America
ISBN   Paperback: 979-8-89091-261-9
ISBN   eBook: 979-8-89091-262-6

All rights reserved. No part of this publication may be reproduced, stored in a retrieval system or transmitted in any way by any means, electronic, mechanical, photocopy, recording or otherwise without the prior permission of the author except as provided by USA copyright law.

The opinions expressed by the author are not necessarily those of ReadersMagnet, LLC.

ReadersMagnet, LLC
10620 Treena Street, Suite 230 | San Diego, California, 92131 USA
1.619. 354. 2643 | www.readersmagnet.com

Cover design by Will Hobbs
Interior design by Don De Guzman

DEDICATION

This compilation of miracle stories is written for my three wonderful sons—Charles II, Trevis, and Desmond—and my eight grandchildren—Jenee', Tiana, Royale, TJ, Christion, Deion, Jasmine and Kayla. Also my beautiful great granddaughter, Aryale —and two grandchildren by marriage, Jonea and Monay. Thank you for the joy you have brought into my life from the day I first held each of you in my arms until this very day. You have made me so proud of the men and women you have become. Our times together have brought fun, laughter, and joy into my life. My thanks to my daughters-in-law, Minna, Maureen and Virginia. Thank you for being devoted wives, mothers, and daughters-in law. You are beautiful, intelligent role models for my grandchildren.

This book is also dedicated to my mother, Hazel Walker, though she is now in Heaven with God. Everything I am or ever hope to be is because of her guidance and unwavering love. She taught me about God's unconditional love, which gave me the strength to endure and survive many life experiences.

This dedication is also to my two wonderful sisters, Elizabeth who now have joined the angels in Heaven and my sister, Deloris who has always been there for me every step of the way. I love them dearly.

INTRODUCTION

As I approach my twilight years, I feel an imperative to witness to as many people as I can before I enter those pearly gates with my Lord and Savior, Jesus Christ. I started talking about Miracles in 2011 when God impressed upon me to write my memoir, "Cuddled in God's Hands." To be honest, I retired from education after 39 years in 2009. I was a teacher, a vice principal, a principal, a trainer of trainers in over 20 fields of study. I had studied under the best trainers and had trained teachers with a team called the B.O.L.T Team before I retired. I had every confidence that I was prepared for my after-retirement life. Surely, my intentions were to one day use that knowledge to train principals, teachers, and staff to be the best in that field of study. However, after I retired, I realized that the job had taken a physical toll on my body. I was exhausted. I heard God telling me to rest and not do anything until he summoned me. And so, I did not do anything until one night I heard God summoning me to write some things down about my life. He began urging me, nudging me in my sleep until I began to get up and write down some things in my notebook which I always kept for ideas and recipes.

    As I began writing my thoughts, I felt God's presence increasingly each day. Each night, ideas about my childhood flooded my mind to things I had completely forgotten. Some of my memories were traumatic like remembering how my mom would tell me how my father had been killed in a car accident when I was a year and a half. That incident helped to shape my life. It left an indelible print on my mind. Many memories were happy and exciting like eating at the best home cooked meals especially prepared by my southern mother. Golden fried chicken, potato salad, macaroni and cheese, fried corn, fluffy buttermilk biscuits and gravy, collard greens and cornbread, homemade vanilla ice cream, coconut cake, butter pound cake, apple pie danced in my head. I could smell the aroma permeating in my senses as I wrote my thoughts down.

More memories flowed from my mind of all the friends I had and the proms and parties and activities I was involved in like being in the dance troop or being a Tigerette with the marching band and spending time with the speech club, student council and the list go on.

The book explores my earliest exposure to racism, prejudice, segregation, and Jim Crow Laws. It gives details into experiences which show the evil of this type of crime against humanity. No child should be brought up under those oppressive circumstances.

Some nights, I could not sleep because God would wake me out of a sound sleep. He wanted me to talk about an incident which happened to me at the time over 25 years before. It was the beginning of my belief in Miracles. It was the night I gave my life fully to God. I was at my lowest point in life. I had left my oppressive husband of 18 years with my three sons not knowing where I was going or what I was going to do. God came to me in a vision. I heard the voice of God telepathically. He assured me that everything was going to be all right if I just followed and believed in him. The details of this vision will be shared in chapters to follow.

"Cuddled in God's Hands" was my first book about Miracles, visions, wonders, and supernatural occurrences. But this new book will be a compilation of three of my books. I decided I would extract all the supernatural events and compile these magnificent stories into one reading. This will be an astonishing book to sit down and sip your favorite tea or coffee or even that mellow sparkling Chardonnay.

You will get to read the mystical stories from my book, "Miracles Blossom from the Spirit Within." While visiting Paris, the Holy Spirit revealed a startling vision telepathically about the real meaning of Miracles and gave detailed instructions on how to attract and recognize Miracles in our everyday lives.

Nothing can prepare you for the last mysterious book I wrote during the worst period of my life. The forbidden word Cancer creeped into my life. This word I never even uttered into the universe. But there it was! In my journal, I daily came face to face with the stark reality that it was taking a toll on my mind and body. The surgery, chemotherapy and radiation occupied my thoughts day and night, but the holy spirit enveloped my being and wrapped me in God's grace and loving arms daily. It brought me through the valley of death and cleansed me free of that dreaded disease. That is why I called this book, "Thank You Jesus, You Never Change." Because here I am eight years later blessed and able to testify that my God is the same yesterday, today and will be tomorrow.

I have never authored a book about the Shekinah Glory although I detailed a supernatural story about it before. In this book, I will take you on a spiritual journey that will awaken your senses to look for and spot it in your everyday pictures and those of others. You will begin to recognize that Mary, the mother of Jesus and Jesus himself is gracing us with his and her presence. Just like when you see the rainbow after the rain and think of God's promise to us that he will never again destroy us again with water, likewise, seeing the Shekinah Glory will remind us that God still sees and hears us.

So are you ready for some intriguing, extraordinary stories! Then put on your seat belt because I am about to take you on a supernatural journey. Buckle up!

CONTENTS

Dedication iii
Introduction iv
Chapter 1:   What Is The Shekinah Glory 1
Chapter 2:   My Beginning Transformation 15
Chapter 3:   What Exactly Are Miracles? 18
Chapter 4:   Steps To Attracting And Recognizing Miracles 23
Chapter 5:   Six Strategies For Attracting Miracles 25
Chapter 6:   Miracle Journal Entry For The Spirit Within 33
Chapter 7:   How To Begin Writing Your Own Journal 36
Chapter 8:   Miracle Discovery Of My Excruciating Pain 42
Chapter 9:   Vision Of My Mother Appearing Like An Angel 52
Chapter 10: Miracle Angel Sign 55
Chapter 11: Miracle Encounter With A Stranger 58
Chapter 12: Phoenix Rising From The Ashes 63
Chapter 13: I Heard The Voice Of God 73
Chapter 14: Paris Trip Vision Revealed 81
Chapter 15: Miracle Stories Told To Me 90
    A. Miracles By M.p East Bay 91
    B. My Miracle Baby 95
    C. In Loving Memory Of My Son 96
    D. Hawaii's Road To Hana 98

CHAPTER 1

What is the Shekinah Glory

> **When the Israelites left Egypt at night, "The Lord went in front of them in a pillar of cloud by day, to lead them along the way, and a pillar of fire by night, to give them light, so that they might travel by day and night. Neither the pillar of cloud by day nor the pillar of fire by night left its place in front of the people.**
>
> **(Exodus 13:21-22)**

I became fascinated with the Shekinah Glory many years ago when I was Principal of Bishop Elementary School. An event happened there which shook me to my very core. The incident was so traumatic yet spiritually awakening that it captivated my senses in another realm. The sixth sense was no longer enough. It tapped into a new consciousness. I will explain later but to delve into this subject I need to explain what I know of The Shekinah Glory.

According to Wikipedia, "The concept is found in Judaism. The Hebrew bible mentions several places where the presence of God was felt and experienced as a Shekinah, including the burning bush and the cloud that rested on Mount Sinai. The Shekinah was often pictured as a cloud or as a pillar of fire and was referred to as the glory of God."

Wikipedia further explains, **"Divine presence of God, inner God or simply presence is a concept in religion, spirituality, and theology that deals with the ability of God to be "present" with human beings."**

My memory of the Shekinah Glory was reignited one day as I sat down to reminisce and took out the family photo album. I opened the album with the birth announcements and pictures. The first photos were of my oldest, Lil Charles as I called him. It had been quite a while since I had looked at these pictures. I smiled and thought of that joyous day when I had held my first-born son which his dad and I had hoped for. Suddenly, something in the picture caught my eye. My mind's eye zoomed in on a part of the picture which I had never captured before. The pictures had red pillars of clouds raining down on Lil Charles' body! Some pictures also had a white cloud directly under his picture as I held him in my arms. What could be so unusual about that you may ask?

This encounter transported me like a time machine back to when I was Principal at Bishop Elementary School. When I came to Bishop, I coined the school's motto, **"The School Where Miracles Happen.** "As you read certain parts of my book, you will understand the significance of that term. I believed it was a miracle for me to have been chosen for that school and that God had placed me there for a reason. The prophecy repeatedly proved true in so many ways. The school excelled in areas no one thought possible. The students, staff and parents were a joy to behold. I had an opened door policy where staff members often stopped by my office during breaks and after school. Usually, I stayed late after school and many staff members stayed late as well. Teachers were always trying to make creative lessons and be ready for their eager learners.

One afternoon, one of my teachers, Julie, stopped by my office just to chat. She had been out ill the week before, and she wanted me to know that she felt better. She thought it was some bug she had caught because it left her tired when she tried to go jogging as she often did. She was a terrific teacher, and she discussed the STAR test coming up and what she was doing to prepare her students. Julie also discussed a little about family life. After a while, she realized the time was getting late, so she excused herself to go back to the classroom to wrap things up so she could get home.

The next morning it started off its usual way with me going out to the cafeteria to watch the children eat their morning breakfast. I chatted with students about their food and classes, and they smiled back at me, and life was good. The bell rang and I walked out to watch the children scatter to their different classrooms. It was always a treat to see them excitedly skip off to class. The teachers greeted them gleefully at the door. What a wonderful day it was!

Then in a flash, my world turned upside down. In fact, the whole school's world turned upside down. My secretary came into my office. She seemed shaken and nervous. She said Julie's husband was in the office and he said he needed to see me and that it was especially important. He came in and sat down in a melancholy manner. He said Julie was on life support in the hospital! My heart raced and at first, I couldn't comprehend. He talked on about when she got home from school the day before, she went down to the mailbox and fainted. They took her to the hospital. Something was wrong with her heart. Maybe it had been there since birth, but they had not discovered it before then. He kept talking but my head was swirling. He left and I was in a state of shock and disbelief.

Several days later, he called to say she had been taken off life support and pronounced brain dead. Unbelievable sadness enveloped me and the entire staff. Then my role as the consoler in chief began. What needs to be done? What do we do with her students? How do we tell her students, staff and parents? I called a staff meeting and told the teachers. The crying and sadness were tremendous. I asked the 5th grade team which Julie was a member of to stay behind so we could strategize on next steps.

AS difficult as it was, this extraordinary group of teachers came together as a dynamic team. They discussed how they would handle nurturing and keeping her students engaged in learning just as Julie would expect. We hired a substitute and the team worked out a schedule to keep the students engaged and consoled. My vice principal was extremely helpful, and we worked tirelessly to keep the rest of the school progressing as we dealt with this tremendous tragedy. We also hired grief counselors to be available for any student who needed them and to talk to all the students. The district office gave us permission to get any help necessary. My superintendent was especially helpful and thoughtful, making sure we were all okay. The days after that were difficult. I had to manage the school's business and keep everyone's morale up. I hired a substitute teacher to take over Julie's class. I stopped by occasionally to check on the students to see how they were doing. One day my secretary came into my office and said the substitute teacher wanted me to come down to the classroom to see something special the students had prepared. For some reason, I grabbed my camera and took it with me. To my surprise, the students were dressed up as characters in a play they were reading. They had made their costumes from Newspapers. I was so proud of them! I told them how proud of them I was and asked if I could take their pictures. During those days, some parents objected to their child's pictures being taken so it was important to ask. They excitedly said yes. Weeks later, I developed the pictures. I became upset as I scrolled through them. Some were filled with total red blobs but no pictures. Others were filled with white cloud like streaks across the students' bodies. Then there were some absolutely perfect. I took them in succession so I couldn't understand how some were messed up and others were not. I even threw a few in the trash can.

Pat, one of my teachers, stopped by as I was looking through the pictures. She saw that I was upset and asked me if she could see the pictures. As she looked at the pictures, her eyes widened, and she exclaimed that she wanted to take the pictures with her to her church that night. She saw something in those pictures that looked familiar. The next day, Pat came rushing into my office early out of breath. "What's wrong? I asked. She told me that she had gone to a Catholic mass the night before. After service, she talked to the priest about what had happened to Julie and showed him the pictures of Julie's students. The priest gasped. The priest was astonished! He said the pictures showed that there was a supernatural presence in that classroom, and it was the Virgin Mary. He told her Mary sometimes shows herself in pillows of clouds. Sometimes the clouds were red, white, black or blue.

The priest showed Pat this tattered book which appeared to have been used a lot. It had pictures like in Julie's class. The book was titled, **"A Scientist Researches Mary, the Ark of the Covenant."** I took the book home and read it with a new understanding and felt enlightened and connected to a higher power. This priest had taken pictures all over the world. He was skeptical at first, being a scientist, but he soon discovered that as he took pictures of all the holy statues where Mary had been seen and adored, some showed white lights on them. He took more pictures of holy relics and more lights of assorted colors sizes and shapes formed on pictures. He was in awe of these beams of light, and he began to know that he was in the presence of something holy and righteous. The lights represented God's presence and was symbolic that God's lights or beams meant that he was near and always around us. In time of trouble or happiness, he shines in our lives. What an awakening that was! To think that God's presence or Mary's had visited Julie's students. After that, teachers brought me pictures of students all over the school doing musicals, walkathons and daily activities and they all had the white light or as we know it now, the Shekinah Glory around them.

We decided to have a memorial service at school. Everyone came together to make the memorial so very special. It was a sight to behold. The school's motto rang loud and clear that day. It truly was **The School Where Miracles Happen**. We invited Julie's parents and husband. The whole school came out to the field behind the school and together we read poems and recited memories and said silent prayers. We had the district to send over a crew which helped us plant a tree in her memory. It is still there today. Her mother came by my office after the service. I told her what a wonderful teacher Julie was and how her students and parents adored her. Her mother was grateful for the memorial and expressed her gratitude. I had bought the book about Mary and gave her a copy. I had taken pictures of some of the children with the light on them as well. She was ecstatic and filled with emotion. We hugged and said our goodbyes.

As the years passed, I became more spiritual and connected to God in a deeper level. I was more in tune to messages of God. I listened to the holy spirit within me. I became one with God. I became more observant of the pictures with the light. I started telling my family and friends about the light in their pictures. Family and friends would get excited and bring me pictures. Sometimes there were stories behind the pictures with the light on them. Sometimes they would share a story of something that person was going through like they had lost a loved one and the light on them meant God was present. Sometimes I would see a light on a picture of a student and wonder what they were going through.

Often as I scrolled through Facebook, I would see the bold white light across their pictures and wonder what they were experiencing because whatever it was, God was present. There are times when I see the bold white light across a picture of a friend, I will call them and talk about what may be happening in their lives. I called a family pastor when I saw the bold white light on his picture one day on Facebook. He said one of his best friends had died. I saw another picture of a friend on Facebook. She looked happy and was swinging at a park. Soon after that, she became the first black mayor of Tracy. I sent her a note to let her know that God's presence was on her. Now that you know a little about the Shekinah Glory or divine light, you will be thrilled every time you see a picture with the light. I can't wait for you to experience the joy that I feel every time I see a picture. I have included a few pictures in this chapter showing the light on family members and close friends. We need to spread the word to let people know that God is real and ever present in our lives today. When you see the bold white light on your pictures, you will know that God sees you and he is with you. Be on the lookout for the light in your pictures.

Bishop Elementary became a school where Miracles Happened daily! The miracle stories will be featured later in the book. I dedicate the title of my book to Bishop School and the dedicated staff, students, parents, district personnel and all who made the school a family-oriented place. Stay tuned.

SHEKINAH GLORY

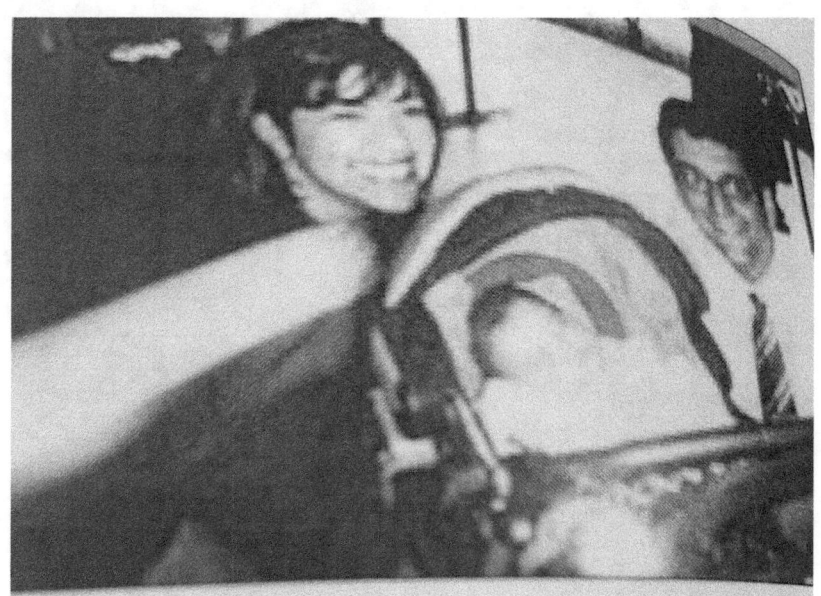

FRANCES PURNELL DAMPIER

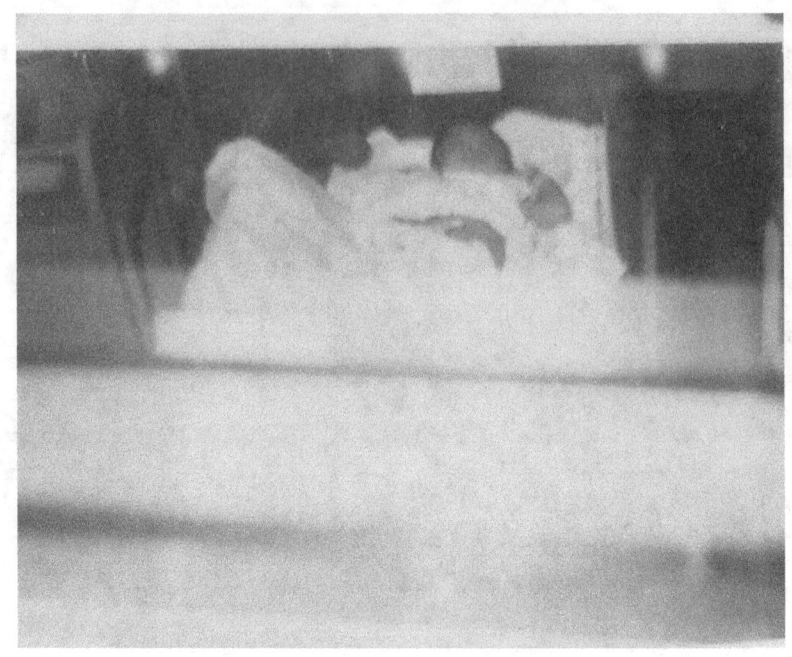

SHEKINAH GLORY

SHEKINAH GLORY

FRANCES PURNELL DAMPIER

SHEKINAH GLORY

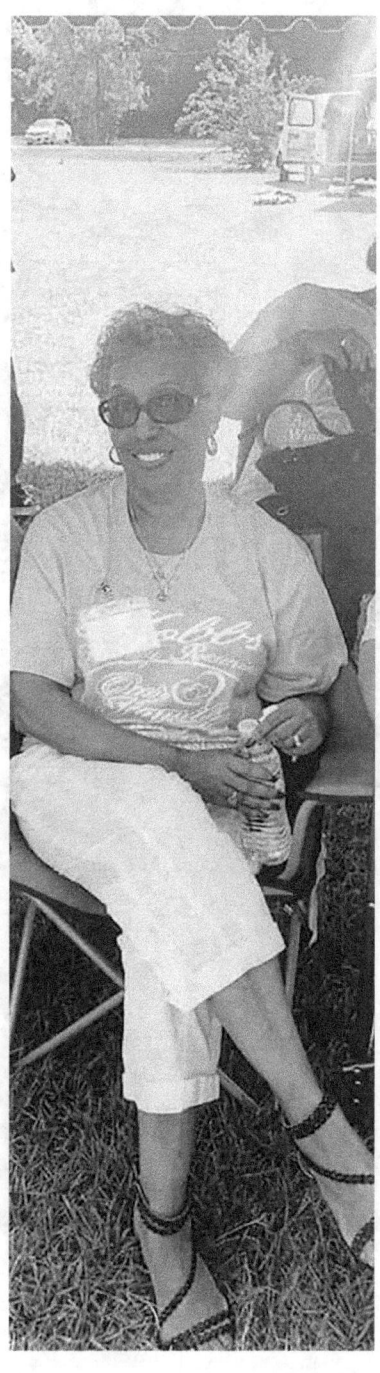

CHAPTER 2

MY Beginning Transformation

When I was twelve years old, I decided to give my life to Christ. I would have done it sooner, but my parents believed I should wait until I was old enough to truly know what I was doing. I had been brought up in the church and knew my bible from going to Sunday School class every Sunday and bible study during the week.

    This Sunday started off like a typical Sunday with the choir singing and once they got everyone rejoicing, the pastor took to the pulpit. As he began preaching, I felt a stirring in my soul which I had not felt before. He finished his sermon and invited people to come to Jesus and give their life to Christ. Before, I knew it, I hurried up to the front filled with the holy spirit and shook the pastor's hands. In those days, you didn't have to attend classes to join church. You became a member and were given the right hand of fellowship. As was customary, your pastor on a certain Sunday after that would baptize you. However, my stepfather was an assistant pastor of New Zion Baptist Church and ministered to his own church, so my pastor gave my stepfather permission to baptize me.

    My stepfather happened to be baptizing some of his new members from his church, Hays Creek Baptist Church so he included me in this group. To my astonishment, the baptism was going to be in a river!! At my church, it was done in an indoor pool. This was scary indeed! I had heard about John the Baptist being baptized in a river and now I too would be given that honor. I felt blessed and exalted. The congregation sang the old hymn, "Take Me to The Waters."

> "Take me to the waters
> Take me to the waters
> Take me to the waters
> To be baptized."

The next thing I remembered was my stepfather holding my back and nose and totally immersing me in the deep waters. When I came up from the waters a feeling of euphoria came over my body. I knew something supernatural had enveloped me and from that day on I became a new creature in Christ. This experience laid the foundation for my strong belief in the Almighty God. My new transformation began on this day.

Speaking in Tongues.......a strange occurrence

Another mystical event happened to me when I was around twelve or thirteen years of age which elevated my belief in God even more. My grandmother wanted to visit her daughter, my mother's sister who lived in Joliet, Illinois. I wanted to go too because my aunt had a daughter who was my age and we always had fun together. I also wanted to go because my Aunt Catherine was the best cook in the world next to my mama. Her cakes were made with pure butter and lots of vanilla. When you bit into the cake, it literally melted into your mouth. It was as smooth as vanilla ice cream. In addition to her cakes, the fried chicken, greens and yams were out of this world. I couldn't get there fast enough. I had such a wonderful time playing with my cousins and going to the amusement park. The rides were thrilling, and the cotton candy and food were incredible.

One day, my aunt announced to everyone that we were all going to a tent revival in Chicago, a nearby city. A Reverend A.A. Allen was going to be there. My aunt was beside herself with glee. She exclaimed what a great preacher he was! Everyone seemed ecstatic but me because I had never heard of him. My Aunt Catherine and all her sisters were members of the Church of God in Christ. My grandmother and mother were Baptist for life. Anyway, I was in for a huge surprise. This preacher started calling people up to the stage who needed healing. People in wheelchairs, crutches, with cancer and other horrible illnesses lined up to be healed. He laid hands on them and miraculously they started throwing away wheelchairs and getting up to walk. People were throwing away walking canes and crutches and walking. Some people started speaking in tongues. I didn't know what they were saying or what was going on. I was caught up in this phenomenon. One person said the devil had possessed her and the pastor called out the devil and supposedly it came out of her, and they threw a towel over it to keep it from getting on other people. The pastor said he had exorcised the devil from her. What in God's name was going on I thought. I was frightened and nervous.

After that, the pastor told the whole congregation to form an extensive line and he was going to lay hands on everybody. Row by row filed out and lined up in the aisle. Then it came to our row. My grandmother who was in front of me went up to the pastor and just like all the folks in front of her, he laid hands on her. She immediately fell as soon as he touched her head. Someone caught her and quickly took her with the others to a prayer room. Scared out of my skin, I ran back to my seat shaking with uncontrollable fear. It seemed like hours later; mother came out of the prayer room. She looked different and was quiet at first. My aunt asked her what had happened in the prayer room. My grandmother said she was on her knees praying when something pulled on her and enveloped her body from head to toe. She started speaking in tongues and the Holy Ghost took over her body. Now this was strange coming from my grandmother who was a Baptist all her life and had never spoken in tongues. She said it was the most exhilarating joyous feeling she had ever experienced. For the first time in her sixty years of age, she felt fulfilled and closer to God. Because of my grandmother, I too felt closer to God. This was probably my first experience with the power of miracles.

CHAPTER 3

WHAT Exactly ARE MIRACLES?

The Holy Bible tells us that a miracle is an unusual happening, one that goes against logic or the normal laws of nature. Miracles are done by the power of God.

Many philosophers and creative thinkers have attempted to answer that question.

Henry Thoreau quoted, **"Could a greater miracle take place than for us to look through each other's eyes for an instant."**

Bernard Berenson quoted, **"Miracles happen to those who believe in them."**

Mother Teresa quoted, **"I prefer you to make mistakes in kindness than work miracles in unkindness."**

Saint Augustine quoted, **"Miracles are not contrary to nature, but only contrary to what we know about nature."**

An anonymous quotes states, **"Miracles are natural. When they do not occur, something has gone wrong."**

Miracles are natural, and thanks to God Almighty they still are happening. The only thing that has gone wrong is our ability to recognize and understand when they occur with us. Have you ever experienced something extraordinary and so implausible and unbelievable that goes against what you know as real and sane? When the event occurred, did you scratch your head in disbelief? Did you toss the event aside as if to say it was impossible and therefore I will pretend it never happened so that people will not consider me crazy or foolish? Have you ever felt a presence and looked around to find nothing there and think, now that's strange. Have you ever been on your way somewhere and a voice in your head said to go back home and once you returned home you noticed that you left the coffee pot on? Did you tell someone about it but instead of saying a voice inside your head told you to turn around and go back, you said, "Something told me to turn around!" Well, that voice was God, Jesus, the Holy Spirit. All of these occurrences are miracles performed by God, Jesus, or the Holy Spirit.

Are you struggling in your belief in miracles? One of my favorite quotes states, **"Faith is not believing God can, it is knowing he will."**

When in doubt, there are several things one must do.

Six Strategies for Attracting Miracles

1. Be open to all possibilities.
2. Allow yourself to experience a spiritual awakening.
3. Pray and call on God for guidance and assurances.
4. Draw positive energy into your life. Weed out negativity.
5. Expect a miracle to happen in all circumstances.
6. Make time to meditate daily to attract all that is good and holy.

A Christian should have no trouble believing in miracles because the very word *Christian* means to be Christlike, to be of Christ. The Bible tells us that if we are united in Christ, we are transformed. We are reborn a new creature. The key word is *reborn*. Just as a newborn baby is not fearful of anything, we must also be free to believe and step out on faith in our willingness to experience all that God has to offer. Know that we are new creatures in God and our power is limitless because we are indeed children of the Most High. A favorite mentor, Maya Angelou, once said**, "Stand up straight and realize who you are, that you tower over your circumstances. You are a child of God. Stand up straight."**

Growing up, most Christians have learned about miracles in Sunday School, Bible study, or from the pastor during regular services when he preaches different sermons. The stories in the Old Testament have always been fascinating. The New Testament is even more intriguing, with Jesus arriving on the scene. Jesus actually walked among us and witnessed firsthand the humanness of each of us. He loved everybody no matter what their station was in life; no matter if they were Jews or Gentiles, no matter what their affliction happened to be. He performed miracles to all who were present believers and nonbelievers. God certainly did us a favor when he performed a most perfect miracle and placed Jesus Christ in the womb of our Virgin Mary. Without that miracle, we would undoubtedly all be condemned to a life of eternal sin.

As Christians, when we testify of God's grace and miracles, we honor his name. Sharing miracle stories with others puts a smile, no doubt, on God's face— probably as illuminating as one million times the sun's rays. Three of God's most powerful stories in the Bible explain Jesus' healing and miraculous capabilities.

One such powerful miracle in the Bible comes from the book of John, chapter 2. Jesus was at a wedding with his mother. When the wine was all gone, his mother, Mary, went to Jesus and told him that all of the wine was gone. Jesus looked at his mother and replied**, "Dear woman, why do you involve me? My time has not yet come."** But because Jesus was an obedient son, he told the servants to bring all the available jars. They brought six stone water jars that held from twenty to thirty gallons each. Jesus directed them to fill the jars with water.

Then he said**, "Now draw some of it out and take it to the master of the banquet."** The servants obediently did as they were told and when the master tasted it, the water turned into the most delicious wine the master had ever tasted. In fact, he remarked that someone had been holding out on him. This was the first of Jesus' miraculous signs that he performed at Cana. He thus revealed his glory, and the disciples in Galilee began to put unyielding faith in him.

John 4:43-54 tells us of a moving story of one of these heartwarming miracles. This second story explains that Jesus was visiting Cana in Galilee, where he had performed miracles before. The Galileans knew of his miracles and the word of what he was capable of doing in terms of healing was known all over the region. An official in Capernaum heard that Jesus was in Galilee and went to him and begged Jesus to come with him in order to heal his son, who was very ill.

The worried father was insistent that Jesus honor his request because he feared his son was near death. Interestingly, Jesus said to him, **"Unless you people see miraculous signs and wonders, you will never believe."**

The official wasn't necessarily focusing on what Jesus was trying to tell him because he had his son on his mind. Jesus no doubt shocked him when he told him to go back to Capernaum. Jesus declared to him, **"You may go. Your son will live!"** The scriptures say the man took Jesus at his word and headed back to Capernaum, which was about twenty miles from Galilee. While the man was on his way back home, his servants met him with the news that his son was alive and doing well. The royal official asked the servants if they could tell him what time the boy began getting better. The servant replied, "The fever left him yesterday at the seventh hour." The father was shocked because he realized that this was the exact time in which Jesus had said to him, "Your son will live!" Therefore, the Bible tells us that the royal official and everyone in his household believed in Jesus and the power of his miracles.

This third story comes from John, chapter 4. Jesus had left Judea and was on his way back to Galilee. On his way back, he decided to go through Samaria because he and his disciples were thirsty and he knew Jacob had a well there. The disciples left him and went into the city for supplies. Jesus was sitting alone near the well when a Samaritan woman came to draw water. Jesus said to her, "Will you give me a drink?" The Samaritan woman was shocked that Jesus would be associating or talking to her, let alone asking her to draw him some water. The woman said to Jesus, "You are a Jew and I am a Samaritan woman. How can you ask me for a drink?" In those days, Jews and Samaritans did not associate. Jesus answered her, **"If you knew the gift of God and who it is that asks you for a drink, you would have asked him and he would have given you living water."** The woman was confused about this living water Jesus spoke of but Jesus continued to speak to her. He revealed that she had been married five times and that the man she was living with presently was not her husband. This woman knew immediately that she was in the midst of a prophet. Jesus spoke to her about Christ and how he was going to come back one day and take back true Christians to heaven with him. Jesus said to her, **"God is spirit, and his worshipers must worship in spirit and in truth."** And his last words to her were, "I who speak to you am he."

This Samaritan woman became a true believer and went back to town to tell everyone about her encounter with Jesus. Because of her testimony, many people in town were converted and became true believers.

These three stories teach us the true meaning of why it is necessary to reveal how Jesus has intervened in our everyday lives today to perform miracles. Jesus doesn't necessarily want to have to perform miracles in order to convert us but as he said to the royal official, **"Unless you people see miraculous signs and wonders, you will never believe."** It then becomes imperative to recognize and exclaim to those who have doubt that Jesus is who he says he is and that he is our savior and our salvation. Jesus will not reveal himself to us unless we open our hearts to his infinite possibilities. Our five senses are not enough to understand the infinite degree of all that God is. It is important, therefore, to remember the recipes for attracting miracles as described earlier in the chapter. If we allow ourselves to listen to the Holy Spirit within us, then we will experience God's miracles and all that God has in store for us.

CHAPTER 4

Steps to Attracting and RECOGNIZING MIRACLES

Attracting miracles is a unique and intentional skill. Several strategies must occur in order for miracles to be recognizable and consistent in everyday living. The dictionary gives many remarkable definitions of the word *attract*. *Attract* means to evoke, unite, allure, pull, entice, charm, or draw nearby physical force, sensation, or senses. A combination of all or some of these things enables us to experience the awesome power of miracles or blessings from the Holy Spirit. Crediting God for the enchanting masterpiece he has already blessed us with is the first step. Take a look at just one of God's magnificent creatures. Because I have always held a fascination with butterflies as a child, I marvel at the intricate design of these insects. The monarch butterfly is extremely intriguing. The gigantic wings display orange with black veins running throughout its span. The outer edge of the wing has a thick black velvet border that appears to be perfectly symmetrical. Within the black borders are carefully placed white cylindrical spots arranged in an exact arc around the pattern design of dark and light blocks, whose appearance is that of a precise U, forming the body of the wing. The tip of the wing has bright orange, black, and white colors shaped in a perfect V formation. Looking intently at this magnificent insect assures me that God has powers beyond what a mere mortal can comprehend. Take this one insect and multiply it by the hundreds, thousands, or millions of other insects, animals, flowers, trees, fish, fowl, and human beings on the place called Earth and tell me that our God has not created a magical paradise for us, or as I like to call them, *miracles*.

Remember the book of Genesis 1:1-3, **"In the beginning God created the heavens and the earth. Now the earth was formless and empty, darkness was over the surface of the deep, and the Spirit of God was hovering over the waters."**

Imagine this world empty and void of all the beauty we see in nature today. How sad that would be. Therefore, as a first step to attracting more miracles, we must acknowledge and affirm that God has already provided us with the miraculous world in which we live. We must view our world through new prisms, realizing God's grace and love for us already.

The next step in our spiritual journey is to begin practicing some easy steps or strategies in our everyday walk with God. In our daily prayers, we must ask God to help us as we strive to implement the strategies outlined in this chapter.

CHAPTER 5

Six Strategies for Attracting Miracles

*Step 1: **Be open to possibilities***

In order to believe and recognize miracles, we need to tap into our sixth sense. We all possess the ability but we close our minds to anything we cannot understand using our five senses. Using the sixth sense enables us to perceive the dimension of the unseen world of angels, ghosts, signs, symbols, and especially perceptions. This ability to activate the sixth sense helps in our spiritual growth. We can develop this spirituality over time by praying for enlightenment and always being present in the moment, expecting the unexpected and being accepting of odd and unusual circumstances.

I tell the story of my mother's death in my book, *Cuddled in God's Hands*. My mother died unexpectedly. She wasn't sick or anything. I went to Mississippi in a daze to bury my mother. I went through the services numb and sad beyond words could express. When I returned to California, I couldn't quite wrap my head around the fact that my mother was no longer around. Several times I picked up the phone to call her when I was cooking to ask her if she put sour cream in the "sock it to me" cake to make it so delicious and moist. But as I dialed the number, I quickly realized that she wasn't going to answer on the other end. My sadness enveloped me in a deep, depressing way.

One night as I lay sleeping, I woke up feeling a presence in the room. I sat up in bed, and to my astonishment there stood my mother at the foot of my bed. At first, she was standing at the right corner of my bed. She was dressed all in white, but it was as if the sparkles emanated from her and her radiance shined all around her. She looked like a beautiful angel. Through telepathy, my mother spoke to me. "Don't worry about me. I am with God. I am in a better place now and in peace. Remember, God needs angels too."

This vision left me shaken and with a greater inner peace, but also a sense of "knowing" that I had experience something supernatural. I had heard my elders speak of ghosts when I was a child as if it was commonplace, but I didn't expect I would ever experience it. This was a miracle of the best kind for me, a visit from my mother. After that, I was open to many possibilities. Anything was possible if you just believed. God's grace gave me the opportunity to see my wonderful mother again, and I was eternally grateful and appreciative to be a child of the most high.

Step 2: *Allow yourself to experience a spiritual awakening*

Reading spiritual materials and the Holy Bible can help to reveal if you are getting closer to spiritual awakening. It doesn't come overnight. It can take years to tap into this level of consciousness. From my reading, spiritual awakening means to understand your truth. It is an ability to know yourself in a way outside of the normal way people see you. Some authors call it spirit consciousness and being present in all that you do. This is undoubtedly a unique way of attracting a renewal of positive energy. Being spiritual is different from being religious. I was brought up in a religious environment. My stepfather was a Baptist minister. My mother was a member of the women's deacons. We attended church every Sunday not once, but twice. Rising early on Sunday morning, we rushed off to Sunday school. We learned the children's version of biblical stories. Later, we went to regular service and I heard my stepfather give a rousing sermon about Moses, Abraham, King Solomon, or the many miracles of Jesus Christ. In the evening, we gathered again for what we called night service. The choir sang spirituals until everyone became "happy," which meant people were filled with the Holy Spirit. Church members shouted and cried until an usher came over to fan them to calm them down. In the Baptist church, when the Holy

Spirit came upon you, the ushers fanned and fanned. But sometimes we went to the Church of God in Christ. I noticed a difference when church members were overcome with the Holy Spirit. Members shouted, jumped up and down, ran up and down the aisle, and no one touched them. Sometimes they would swirl around and around like a whirlwind, turning and turning. But then something magical would happen to them. They would begin speaking in tongues. I knew something special was going on with these people. They entered another level of consciousness with God. They stepped into an alternative space that went beyond what we know as our reality. They shed the religion and entered into a spiritual realm with God. There in that realm they were able to connect with God on a whole different level. These souls had tapped into an unknown space.

Watching Oprah's "Super Soul Sunday," I was privileged to hear a conversation with Panache Desai. He pretty much summed up what I was attempting to say, **"There's no greater power than to be in harmony with oneself."**

Step 3: *Pray and call on God for guidance and assurance*

Prayer no doubt changes things in a mighty way. Many studies are being made about the benefits of praying. These studies point out that if you pray a few times a day consistently you can prevent memory loss, Alzheimer's, stress, heart attack, anxiety, and depression, to name a few. Well, that certainly is better than exercising. That fits right into my schedule. God waits for our prayer. He loves it when we connect with him in such a personal way. Some people pray only when they are in trouble, but we must pray in good times and in bad times. Blessings and miracles become abundant and commonplace when we are unselfish and honor God all of the time. For me, miracles are so natural and frequent that throughout my day I thank God and praise his name on a continuous basis.

Worshipping and praying with fellow Christians strengthens your bond and connectedness with God. The more people pray collectively to God, the more explosive the power of the prayer. I have heard of many healings when prayer chains are activated. My mother's sister had two different cancers at the same time. She was given six months to live. Her husband was a minister and asked all the churches to pray collectively for her. After a while she went back to the doctor and they could find no trace of the cancer. That was over twenty-five years ago and she is still living and praising God. In Matthew 18:20, Jesus said, "For where two or three come together in my name, then I am in the midst of them."

Step 4: *Draw positive energy into your life*

In order to attract positives, you must weed out the negatives. Negative people and thoughts deplete your energy. Negativity causes self-doubt, unhappiness, and can crush your joy and inner wellbeing. People who think positively do not let negative things get them down. They expect good things to happen to them and good things do occur because they almost will them into being. To attract miracles and positive energy, you must have an optimistic view of the world around you. Sometimes it is difficult to be cheerful and optimistic. This is when you must push through your misery and pull that renewal energy back to the surface. I remember when I was a teacher, being a wife and mother of three boys sometimes would drain me of my energy over the weekend, especially if the family spent the weekend on a family outing, as was usually the case.

Being drained of most of my energy, I knew I had to be alert and ready for action on Monday morning. Middle school students going through puberty expected fun and exciting, motivating lessons. In an attempt to regain much needed energy, I would do two things. First, I had this incredible beautiful red dress that was very flattering. Whenever I wore it, I got tons of compliments from the staff, which helped lift my spirits before I even got to my first period class, so I went into my closet and pulled out the red dress. Next, I pulled out my no-fail lesson plan: a popcorn treat for students. If all students turned in homework the week before, they were promised a popcorn party. I began the day with sustained silent reading from their novels. While they read, I quietly went to the back of the room, turned on the popcorn machine, and filled thirty-two bags of popcorn to the brim.

While they quietly read, I stopped by each desk and handed them a popcorn snack to actually eat while they read. Their eyes looked at me with adoration and gratitude. That started each period on a positive note and the rest of the period went absolutely wonderful. The students were so happy and content that by the end of the day, I felt invigorated myself and ready for the rest of the week.

Step 5: **Expect a miracle to happen in all circumstances**

> **"Jesus loves me**
> **This I know**
> **For the Bible**
> **Tells me so"**

Singing this song during Sunday-school class for children cemented early in my young mind that Jesus loved me and would take care of me no matter what. There was never a doubt that when trouble came my way God would watch over me. My mother, a deaconess, and my stepfather, a minister, never let me forget that God had protected me by pouring out his "blessing" on me. My stepfather often preached about God's magnificent grace. He would have the congregation recite "I am a child of God" several times in unison. Surely, he would say, "If you are a child of the most high, he would never forsake you in your times of need."

Because of these early teachings, I was certain that God favored me and would take care of me always. As I became older and more understanding of my relationship with

God in a deeper, more spiritual way, the word "blessing" evolved into the word *miracle*. To me, the words are synonymous and more in tune with modern-day thinking and philosophies. Whatever term you use, it is clear that God, Jesus, or the Holy Spirit is omnipotent and intervenes on our behalf each day. When the intervention occurs, a miracle or blessing has certainly occurred!

Second nature to me is recognizing all the miracles that envelop my life. Take for example my first ever trip to New York. After retirement, I developed a bucket list of places I wanted to travel to. As luck would have it—or as some would say, unluckily— the first available timeslot for my timeshare was in March. The only timeshare close to New York was located in Atlantic City, New Jersey. That was a lucky break for me, or should I say, miracle, because I loved playing the slots. I invited my best friend and younger sister to come along. They were excited about the trip, but they both chided me, saying the weather was going to be freezing. For some reason, the Holy Spirit kept telling me not to worry about the weather conditions, so I quickly retorted back to them that the weather was going to be fine. Of course, they did not believe me because they had both been to New York before and I had not. For me, I was stepping out on faith alone.

When we arrived in Atlantic City, it was a little chilly. We went shopping to get hats and scarves. There were blocks of high-end stores and fabulous bargains to boot. When a cold breeze crossed our paths, my sister and girlfriend looked at me with the "I told you so" affirmations. The timeshare was absolutely gorgeous, overlooking the New Jersey boardwalk. Looking back now, a year later, I consider it a miracle that we were able to see that beautiful landscape before the disastrous hurricane Sandy totaled it.

We became quite adventurous and decided to take a Greyhound bus to New York, something we hadn't done since our college days. Making it safely to the Big Apple was a real treat. Walking off the bus was an incredible surprise. The weather was spectacular. In fact, it was seventy-three degrees and my sister and friend looked at me in amazement. Of course, I said, "Miracle!" Arriving at the New Yorker Hotel was another miracle, because it was within walking distance of all the marvelous sights.

The day after we arrived, we decided to look for this well-known restaurant where they make breakfast items sculpted like exotic flowers. Striking out walking with a map at our side, we walked and walked. When we arrived near the address of the restaurant, we surveyed the buildings but could not spot the restaurant's sign. We walked up and down the street, and when we were totally disappointed, my best friend's daughter, who had joined us, decided to look up the restaurant on her BlackBerry. To our amazement, she shouted, "It's inside a hotel. Let's look for the hotel!" Suddenly we turned around, and to our amazement, the restaurant was right in front of us. Again, I shouted, "It's a miracle."

Step 6: ***Make time to meditate daily to attract all that is good and holy***

Meditation is a natural way to get in touch with your inner spirit. Taking a little time each day to meditate is important even if it's five or ten minutes a day. Meditating helps to focus and concentrate, enabling us to make more intelligent decisions. It helps to ground or center our thoughts on the Holy Spirit and clears the mind of mundane daily activities.

For three years, I spent three days a week taking yoga classes at my local gym. Yoga is a great way to connect the mind, body, and spirit. It has a way of clearing the mind and balancing the body. Yoga is intended to provide inner calmness and serenity. Oftentimes, I would stop by the gym after work to relieve the inner stresses of the workday. The yoga techniques of proper breathing through meditation and posture exercises helped release anxiety and tension in the body. We did different stretches, poses, and counting as we held stances for a certain number of seconds.

These stretches helped me to learn control of breathing, which in real life came in handy when situations occurred at work. Instead of reacting right away to a crisis, I learned to breathe first more slowly to decrease my heart rate, thereby enabling me to make a more decisive, well-thought-out proactive response. Yoga, I found, is a great prescription for being balanced physically, mentally, emotionally, and spiritually. Yoga is only one way to achieve this meditative process. It is important for each person to find their own avenue to successful meditation. The most important factor in all of this is to find more ways to tune in to the Spirit within each of us.

When I think of God's Miracles, I think of...
(Poem)

Glittering unearthed diamonds
Crystal shimmering lakes
Cascading aromatherapy oil messages
Crying newborn babies
Lush green rainforests
Twinkling shooting stars
Radiant yellow sun rays
Chirping blue birds
Swaying yellow daffodils
Flittering multicolored butterflies
Crashing stormy seas
Bold, striking sunsets
Crimson red roses
Silky, smooth white gardenia petals
Scintillating, bright stars
Iridescent, colorful rainbows
Snowcapped mountains
Mighty majestic eagles
Fresh honeysuckle summer's air
Pure white driven snow
Intense blue skies
Dancing field of swaying flowers
Thirsty humans seeking wisdom
Unseen angels, spirits and beloved departed souls.

By Frances Purnell-Dampier

CHAPTER 6

Miracle Journal Entry for the Spirit Within

Day 1: Today_____, I'm going to enjoy God's kisses for they invoke joy to my soul and remind me that God loves and cares for me. I will listen for the "God Whispers" from the Holy Spirit for he will lead me to do what is right and just. This journal entry is a testimony to God of the miracle he blessed me with on this glorious day.

Set it Up: Explain where you were when the event happened and who was with you unless you were alone.

_____

_____

_____

_____

_____

Tell the Miracles: Be precise, concise and give sequential details.

_____

_____

_____

_____

_____

Recognize the Miracle: Did you know right away that you were experiencing a miracle?

_____

_____

_____

_____

_____

Go tell it: Make sure you tell someone about your miracle while your joy is infectious.

_____

_____

_____

_____

Praise God: Thank God Almighty for blessing you with this glorious gift.

_____

_____

_____

_____

_____

Write it Down: Keep a daily diary each day no matter how small the miracle. If you woke up today, start writing that as your first miracle of the day.

_____

_____

_____

_____

_____

"Every hour God looks after you."

2: Thessalonians 3:3

"Every minute God cares for you."

CHAPTER 7

How to Begin Writing Your Own Journal

J ournaling is a unique way of expressing how Miracles Blossom in your life and how the Holy Spirit led you to all of your incredible miracles. It is not only therapeutic but also spiritually invigorating. T. D. Jakes once said, **"Keep journaling throughout your life. Record the events of your life, the revelations God gives you, and every way God shepherds you into new phases and opportunities."** I totally agree with his incredible insight. In this chapter, I will provide an actual event to guide you as you begin your own twenty-one-day journal. At the end of the twenty-one days, I guarantee you will become more in tune to God's interventions in your daily life. Your spirit will be rejuvenated! Let's begin.

Day 1: Today (insert month, day, year), I'm going to enjoy God's kisses, for they invoke joy to my soul and remind me that God loves and cares for me. I will listen for the "God Whispers" from the Holy Spirit, for he will lead me to do what is right and just. This journal entry is a testimony to God of the miracle he blessed me with on this glorious day.

Set it up: Explain where you were when the event happened and who was with you unless you were alone.

Friday morning, January 18, 2013. I was alone.

<u>*Tell the miracle:*</u>

Today, I had a follow-up pap test appointment at Kaiser Permanente. Six months earlier, at a routine appointment the gynecologist had noticed some abnormities in the test result sample. She had set up a return appointment for today to recheck me as a precautionary measure. I wasn't really worried, because I had never had an abnormal pap test, nor did I feel any different health wise. Usually, I pray to God to take away any harmful health issues before going in and today was no exception. Gathering up my appointment card and my purse, I hastily headed for my car. It was 10:15, so I had plenty of time to get to my 10:30 appointment because Kaiser was only ten minutes away.

As usual, I grabbed my keychain and pushed down on the car remote, expecting to hear the unlocking sound of the car door. No sound came. I pushed every button on the car remote but there was no sound at all. Suddenly, I remembered the old-fashioned way of entering the car, so I put the key in the car door. Aha, I thought, silly me. Now I'm on my way! I put the key in the ignition but there was not even a simple turning over of the engine—dead silence. Thoughts swirled through my head of what next steps to do. I looked up at the sky and said, "Lord, this is not one of my miracles. What should I do?" In an instant, the Holy Spirit told me to call Tracy Toyota. I thought to myself, why am I calling Toyota and not Geico, my car insurance company? But the Holy Spirit led me back into the house and I dialed Toyota's service department. The receptionist answered and I asked for the service department. She transferred the call immediately. I didn't know exactly why I was calling but I felt assured the Holy Spirit knew the reason. Not soon after, the phone rang and rang but nobody answered. I looked at the clock; it was 10:35. Uh-oh, I knew I was late for the appointment. Wondering what to do next, the Holy Spirit led me to call Kaiser to tell them of my dilemma. The nurse asked me if I wanted to cancel and reschedule. I asked if there was a later appointment time and she said no, but to my surprise she said I could come in and wait and if they could they would slip me in between appointments. What? I had been a member for forty years and no one had told me that. So I said

I'd come over as soon as I could. She reminded me that it might be a long wait but I didn't care at that point.

Settling down, I decided that I'd better called Geico and picked up the phone to dial them, but the Holy Spirit turned my sight to the phone number I had written down for Tracy Toyota instead. Instantly, I dialed their number, thinking why am I doing this again. The receptionist answered again, but this time I blurted out about my car problems and my doctor's appointment and somehow I guess she felt sympathy for me. She instantly told me to wait until she got back. She was actually going to walk over to the service department to see if she could find a service attendant. When she returned to the phone, she assured me that she had found someone who could assist me. Wow, was I surprised! The service attendant answered and I blurted out my entire predicament, the car not starting and the doctor's appointment. He said it sounded like my car's battery was the issue. I told him that the car was only four years old. He assured me that it was either the battery or an alternator problem and suggested I call my insurance company. He asked if I had car insurance. I told him I did and was about to hang up when he said, "Wait, where do you live?" I told him my address, and to my amazement he replied, "I'll come over there in about fifteen minutes and bring my jumper equipment. Is that too long?" "Shucks no." I was thinking, whoever heard of a mechanic coming to your house? Perfectly stunned, I told him that I would be waiting for him.

Fifteen minutes later, the service attendant arrived with his jumper machine and the car started up immediately. He advised me to drive on the freeway first to get the juices flowing again. He surprisingly told me his schedule for the whole day and said if I needed him again to call him. Then he reached in his pocket and pulled out his business card and handed it to me. As he was getting in his car, I glanced down at the business card: Director of Fixed Operations/Tracy Toyota. My eyes welled up and I beckoned for him to roll down his window. I said, "Thank you so much for taking the time from your busy schedule to take care of me. You must be my guardian angel." A wide grin crossed his face and he said, "No problem, ma'am, anytime. Call me if you need me today."

Certain that God had intervened and performed a great miracle, I drove the long way to Kaiser and went straight to my gynecologist's office. I began my appointment with the usual filling out of paperwork and the nurse ushering me to take my blood pressure before seeing my doctor. When she took my blood pressure, I could tell something was wrong, because she immediately stammered that she needed to take it a second time. I asked if something was wrong with the first test. She didn't answer, so I started telling her about my car problems earlier. That seemed to relieve her fears, so she took me into the doctor's office.

The doctor asked me about my blood pressure medication and I assured her that I was taking it daily. She said that she still wanted me to take another test after her pelvic examination. She proceeded to do her pelvic exam and breast exam. She assured me that the pap test was probably nothing to worry about and advised that I would get results in two to three weeks. After the consultation, the doctor asked me to retake the blood pressure test with the nurse before leaving. When I took the test again, the nurse's eyes got large and she went to get her supervisor. I knew this wasn't a good sign. When the supervisor came and took the test again, she immediately responded that we were going to have to go over to the medical department and meet with a doctor. Now I knew this was serious, so I told her that I wanted to know right then and there what my blood pressure reading was! She told me that it was 186 over 103. I knew the normal reading was around 125 over 80. To calm their fears, I told them that I had been taking a green bean herbal supplement but I researched it and found no side effects. That didn't seem to calm them down one bit, so they ushered me over to the medical department's waiting room. Meanwhile, I was beginning to understand the seriousness of this problem. I called my own doctor, who was at another Kaiser facility, and told his nurse what had occurred. She told me that my doctor would call me in fifteen minutes. Meanwhile, the supervisor nurse took me into the doctor's office, where they were trying to decide whether to put me on some medication to bring down my pressure or send me to the hospital. Luckily, my own physician called and we decided to increase my medication over a period of a few weeks and to take a blood test to see if the medication was working effectively.

He said I was lucky that I happened to be in the doctor's office when my blood pressure skyrocketed because it was at stroke level.

Recognize the miracle:

I thought to myself that was not luck or coincidence. The entire day was a miracle. I didn't know it at the time, but I was lucky the car didn't start because it made me late for my appointment. The nurse said there had been a lot of people before I came, but I didn't get there until right before lunch, so the office had cleared out and they had no one there but me to look after when I arrived. The mechanic who helped me was God's angel, because if I had called Geico, it would have taken one or more hours for them to get to me, and most of all, I had no idea that my blood pressure was so high. It was through God's miracle that on this specific day he made sure that I was in the right place with medical doctors and services readily available for me, a child of the most high. Wow! How mind-blowing is this miracle? My God is indeed all powerful and all knowing.

Go tell it:

God wants us to go tell someone when he blesses us. The mere excitement in our voices when we blurt out the miracle can convince another person. Sometimes they will tell you a similar story, which confirms to them that their story is credible and indeed a miracle from God. Immediately, I called my sons to tell them what had occurred. They were very concerned but no match for my rambling on and on about God's miracle in the whole process. Later, I told every person I spoke with on the phone who would listen.

Praise God:

I thanked God for letting me be the recipient of such a glorious gift. As always, I usually get teary-eyed when God blesses me in such a magnificent way. Just the mere thought of what he did on one magnificent day in my life makes me so proud to be one of God's disciples. I thanked him for giving me the gift of the Holy Spirit within me to abide and guide me in my daily life's journeys.

Write it down:

    Keeping a journal for me is a way to affirm God's miracles, but also a way of having a record to look back on when things get tough and when troubled times occur in life. Sometimes we are burdened with things that seem too heavy to bear alone and we can turn back a few pages in our journal and know that God was there with us the whole time. My favorite poem is "Footprints." Sometimes I read it over and over. The words are so comforting. When we think we are suffering all alone, God's words echo to me, "My precious child, I love you and would never leave you. During your times of trial and suffering, when you see only one set of footprints, it was then that I *carried you.*"

CHAPTER 8

Miracle Discovery of my Excruciating Pain

Excerpt from my book, "Thank you Jesus, You Never Change. "I wrote a different daily journal entry to describe my cancer journey. It shows a remarkable way to record God's miracles.

This is the third week after my chemo therapy treatment. Usually, only three days before my next treatment but we are moving my chemo back a week. This will make me go through technically twenty-two days of treatment. Actually not, because no chemo will be taking place. Instead, unexpectantly, I am going to be healing hopefully from this extreme urinary tract infection. This was supposed to be my good week! Usually my appetite has come roaring back and I'm preparing all types of good dishes, but my appetite has been lousy. Also, I usually have lots of energy, but all I've been doing is laying still so as not to experience the tremendous pain. Last night was another painful and sleepless night. When will it end? I was praying for daybreak to arrive. I kept getting the urge to go to the bathroom every 15-20 minutes. I so hated getting up.

There was no comfortable position in bed. I tried my back, my left side and then my right side. Nothing made the pain and urge to go to the bathroom go away. I watched the clock repeatedly waiting for the next time I could take my medicine. Three o'clock finally came and I get to take the Norco and get relief for an hour or so. Daylight arrives and down the stairs I go. At least I can open my eyes and not fumble through the darkness. I am thinking something is not normal here. The Norco isn't working. This pain feels like my vagina is inflamed. I decided to call Kaiser even though today is Saturday. I spoke with a nurse who thought I didn't need stronger antibiotics but that the pain may be from radiation and the total healing may not have taken place because of the infection. She suggested I go to the clinic to emergency or wait till Monday and get a doctor of urologist who specializes in this. I said I'd try to wait until Monday because we need to get to the bottom of this. She made a phone appointment but said he may want me to come in. I can't wait until Monday. Thank you Lord!

Day 1:

    I decided to journal this situation.
    Hallelujah, hallelujah! I actually slept some last night! When I woke up I felt strange. Where am I, I thought! I actually felt disoriented because my body had not felt sleep in days. I woke up with energy. I tried to remember if anything different had occurred the day before and remembered that my baby sister, Lois had said a powerful prayer over the phone when we were talking yesterday. I was telling her how bad I was feeling and she was saying she wished she could do something. Suddenly, without warning, she broke out in the most heart warming healing prayer ever! I believe God and the angels stood up and listened. Prayer changes things. For real. For real!
    Since this was Sunday morning, I decided to listen to my favorite show, "Super Soul Sunday" with Oprah. She has the most spiritually inspiring people ever as guests! Every time I watch someone, I grow more and more spiritual in my soul. She had Paulo Coelho as her special guest. He wrote a book called "The Alchemist," an allegory. It teaches powerful lessons about spiritual truths. Will Smith, Pharrell and others said it changed their lives. I immediately ordered it from Amazon.
    Obviously, feeling a little more energized, I decided to cook something. My mind centered on one of my mom's favorite comfort foods, meatloaf. I found it to be easy to make and delicious. My ingredients include three color bell peppers, onions and celery. Dice

and throw them into the hamburger meat. Season it well. Add one egg and panko crumbs as a binder. Shape it into an oblong shape. Pour tomato sauce or ketchup on top. Place strips of bacon across the top covering completely. Cook 45 minutes to one hour. Very, very tasty. Let's hope this feeling continues. I feel good enough to call my friend who is sick and say a prayer with her. I need to pay it forward. God is my savior. Who could ask for anything more!

Day 2:

Last nights slumber was not as good as Saturdays, but I was able to get minimum sleep. The pain certainly has subsided. Taking the Norco every five hours is really assisting with this. Last night, I finally felt like texting my boys and their wives to give my suggestions for Christmas dinner. What say you guys? Do you want to go traditional with a ham or pot roast with all the trimmings, or do we want chicken, sausage, shrimp and crab gumbo all rolled into one or perhaps a crab boil with similar gumbo ingredients. They each text back enthusiastically with the word "gumbo! " They were actually thrilled because I rarely do gumbo, maybe once every few years and they love it! My middle son, Trevis and his fiancée said they would spend Christmas Eve night so they could wake up and help me prepare! Now that sounded like a winner! Help with the meal! Yes, indeed.

Ring, ring the phone was ringing at 9:30 a.m. I didn't recognize the phone number but luckily I picked up. It was actually the urologist from Manteca. She was supposed to call today at 1:45 p.m. She said she had a little time and took a chance on calling me early. We reviewed my symptoms. I told her that Friday night I was in such pain that I started to go to emergency. That's why I called Saturday morning. I told her that the pain seems to be subsiding for the past two days. I loved her demeanor and laugh. She was very soft spoken and seemed genuinely interested in helping me. She reviewed again all the medicines which had been subscribed.

After going over that, she decided the best course of action at this point was to take another urine test. She thought the previous test, which showed negative for infection didn't seem right. She said after the test, she would decide if I needed to come in for a bladder examination. So I told her that I would go to Kaiser today and have that test done for her. She said she should get the test result by Wednesday and would call me the day after Christmas. I liked her a lot! Meanwhile, yesterday I decided to insert these glycerin suppository laxatives by Top Care, to help with constipation. It takes about four hours for me, but usually I have a bowel movement.

It seems to be working for me because I had a bowel movement last night and this morning. What a relief! I feel lighter and less bloated. My son, Trevis actually bought them for me at the store. No one recommended them, he just thought they might help and they did. This whole thing is trial by error.

Day 3:

Nights are like the walking dead these days. I get up all during the night with my eyes slightly open and my hands out in front to keep me from running into a wall. If someone were filming me, I'd look scary. I thought I would recapture the night a few days ago when I actually fell asleep for a few hours which seems to be something totally out of character these days. At least, I finally seem to have a doctor who is trying to find the cause of this problem. Today the urologist called to tell me that my test results showed bacteria but no infection. We both said that didn't make sense. She wanted me to go to Kaiser tomorrow to get an x-ray. She said the stint they put in me in August might be the problem. Stint! What stint I asked. She said, "You had a stint put in during your operation." I told her that wasn't true and that she was scaring me. She laughed and said not to worry about it, but if it was the stint, she could remove it in her office and I wouldn't have to have another operation. She wanted me to come in Friday to examine me.

After we got off the phone, I called two of my sons who were with me during the whole operation and afterwards. We were on three way when I told them what the doctor said. They both said in unison that they remembered the doctor coming in after the surgery and saying that they had put a stint in when I had the bowel blockage. I'm so glad my boys were with me every step of the way, because I was truly not myself. I really love and appreciate them and their wives and significant other. God is in charge, Oh, how I love the Lord.

This week is 1 of 7 because we pushed the 5th chemo treatment back a week. Now, I can have a Merry Christmas and eat gumbo all day! Praise God!

Day 4:

Waking up to Christmas Eve. Somehow, it doesn't seem like it at all because I have been stuck in the house all of two weeks now. I'm missing out on my sororities Kwanza holiday celebration. A lot of people don't know much about the holiday, but my sorority is trying to keep the African tradition alive. It is always very festive with storytellers, dancers, food and the lighting of candles. We all wear our African garb. Well, next year should be a whole lot better than this year for sure.

So this morning I headed straight for Kaiser to get that x-ray the doctor ordered. By noon, the urologist had emailed to say she had received the x-ray and sure enough there was a stint still inside me. This was unbelievable! She said to come in Friday and she was going to remove it. Thank God for this woman. Later, my daughter in law found an article about the stint. It appears that it may have been placed in me during surgery to drain the urine or something. The article say it is meant to be temporary and not stay in longer than three months. Well, it is the fourth month now and I am wondering why my surgeon did not have me come in to remove it. Maybe he was waiting until the entire chemo treatment was over, but, that would be a whole six months. It really doesn't make a lot of sense. I have been in pain for two weeks and on constant pain medication every five hours during the Christmas season for someone leaving a stint inside my body. I am beginning to get upset about this! Well, getting upset will not help. I should just be happy that God intervened and sent this wonderful smart urologist to help me. I am so thankful to me a child of the most high!

Day 5:

Christmas Day is finally here. I am so excited to get this day going. I took my pain pills so that I could get started on the holiday meal. I decided to cook a combination gumbo, a mixture of chicken, ham, sausage, shrimp and crab. My, my that makes some good gumbo. I proceeded boiling a whole chicken and cut up celery, onions, carrots and sausage to make a stock. I then sautéed bell peppers, all three colors, onion and celery and set aside. Next, I took the legs and thighs and floured them and browned them so that I could make a good rue. Adding a few cans of chicken broth with the rue, sautéed vegetables and a couple cans of stewed tomatoes gave the gumbo a great look. Later, I added crab and lobster. Last, I added seasoning and gumbo file as a thickness. This was going to be some good gumbo. At the end, I cooked corn bread, green salad, rice and my son fried chicken wings. The family came over, Charles and his family and Trevis and his family. We laughed, told family stories and ate until we were stuffed. Oh, and I made an apple pie from scratch for the first time. We ate hot apple pie a la mode. It was so delicious. We all gathered in the living room to open presents. We were overjoyed with all of our gifts. The grandchildren, especially were excited. All in all, it was a beautiful Christmas!

Day 6:

I couldn't sleep last night anticipating my trip to the clinic this morning to get this stint removed.

My son, Trevis and his fiancée, Virginia decided to go with me. When we arrived, we looked on the wall and smiled at each other. There on the wall was a picture of my urologist. I had only spoken with her over the phone, but for some reason, I did not pick up from her voice that she was African American. I knew that God had truly given me an angel. When we entered her office, she explained what she was going to do. She said that she believed in miracles like I did, because some voice told her that the stint might be the culprit after the urine test did not show an infection. I smiled and told her that I called those, "God whispers." My son asked her about why this stint was put in. She explained that during my first surgery, the kidney had a thermal burn and the doctor wanted it to heal before removing it. The problem with that scenario is, I believe, the doctor forgot to take it out. So here I was for over two weeks suffering in extreme pain day and night and having to take pain pills every five hours.

Anyway, the urologist performed the surgery like the pro she was. As she prepared to take out the stint, she asked me to tell her about my book and as I testified, she started pulling the stint out. When I would stop talking, she would say, go on tell me more. In a few minutes I felt this alien like thing being pulled out of me. It was about 10-12 inches long!! It only hurt a little bit too! I asked the doctor if I could hug her and she laughed and said, "Put your pants on and come outside. I'll hug you then." We laughed so hard. Sure enough, when I walked outside fully dressed, she reached out and gave me a big hug. I called her one of God's angels. This is truly one of those times when I prayed to God and said, "Thank you, Jesus. You never change!" He said he would always be with me and he has!

Stint information: Removal

A camera called a cystoscope was inserted after numbing medication is administered. The cystoscope is advanced into the bladder and the stint is grasped with an instrument and removed. Most stints should remain in for no longer than three months. If it is left too long, it can form stones directly on it, making removal difficult.

Day 7:

A new day and a renewed beginning today because Glory to God, the stint has been removed now. My son, Desmond and his family bought me for Christmas an orthopedic pillow which conforms to your head. I slept on that last night and after taking my Motrin went to sleep. I only got up about three times and I urinated so much better. When I got out of bed today though, I felt my whole bottom hurt. I could feel a different kind of pain. I believe it was coming from the inside like where the stint came all the way through my body and out the vagina. Maybe, it needs to heal or something. I am still very upset with my surgeon. I emailed him what my urologist was going to do and I asked him if taking the stint out would cause any more problems with the bowel blockage. The urologist had also emailed him. His stand in doctor, replied because my surgeon was on vacation until January 4th. His stand in emailed me back saying it was fine to take the stint out. I emailed him back yesterday and asked him when it was scheduled for the stint to be taken out. I can't wait for his reply. I'm thinking they forgot. What incompetence! By midday, I decided I needed to eat something, so I made bacon and pancakes. They tasted good. I figure I had better be bad because if all goes well, I'll be back doing chemo again next Tuesday. I'll be back to no appetite and feeling bad or worse for a week and a half. I have to feel better by tomorrow so I can update my family with my daily information. I need at least two days of positivity. Boy this is almost funny!

SUPERNATURAL MIRACLE STORIES

Miracles have always been prevalent in my life. There are so many supernatural occurences. The following stories will leave you flipping page after page with excitement. You will salivate for more of the stories.

CHAPTER 9

Vision of My Mother Appearing Like an Angel

Eight years after my divorce from Charles, my world fell apart again. My sister, Elizabeth called me the day after my birthday, October 23, 1988, screaming that my mother had died of unknown causes, perhaps a heart attack. She had been at church all day, where the women were putting on a skit about Mary Magdalene. My mother played Mary Magdalene and was thrilled about it. My best friend's mother had dropped her off after church and said my mother was laughing and so happy about how the skit had turned out. In those days, neighbors, kept an eye out for the elderly in the community, so when one of them noticed the light still on and the front door open at midnight, she went over to check on my mother. After calling for her and getting no response, the person called my sister, who lived in the same town. When my sister and brother-in-law arrived, they found my mother, lying dead on the bathroom floor. I couldn't think straight, but I promised I would get on the first plane home.

Other than my children, no one meant more to me. My mother had been my mentor, my role model, and my comfort all of my life. I wasn't sure I could survive this. On my way home, I knew I would have to be strong, because both my sisters were going to be too distraught to deal with this situation. We all managed to arrange for the funeral service and comforted each other. My sister Deloris, who had a beautiful voice, sang Mother dear's favorite song at the funeral. The funeral was beautiful, but at the wake the night before, I approached the casket, thinking that if I touched my mother, I would get some sense of peace. Instead, all I felt was a cold, hard body. I cried out, "That's not my mother; that's not my mother." My mother was warm and gentle. She cared about everybody, often taking food to the sick and those who needed help. She taught Sunday school every Sunday and was a deaconess. My mother read her Bible so much that the pages were old, tattered, and falling out. She absolutely loved God. Why was this happening? For the first time, I questioned God. I knew what God had told me. He would be with me always. "Where are you?" I asked.

A few weeks later, after returning to California, another miracle happened. I was sleeping in my bedroom when I felt a presence. I sat up in my bed and looked around. To my amazement, there was my mother, standing at the foot of my bed. At first, she was standing at the far right of the bed. She was dressed all in white, but it was as if sparkles emanated from her and radiance shown around her. She looked like an angel. Her face had a beautiful, soft, smooth glow. My heart raced faster and faster. I couldn't believe my eyes. Could this be my mother coming back to me? She started to move and glide along the foot of the bed. She sat on the left side of the bed. Through telepathy, she spoke to me. *Don't worry about me. I am with God. I am in a better place now and in peace. Remember, God need angels too."* Then she reached toward me, and I heard her say in my mind, *Come, come.* She kept beckoning for me, like she wanted to hold and comfort me. But something was holding me back, and I couldn't break loose. I finally mustered every bit of strength I had and lunged toward my mother. Then I broke loose, unshackled so to speak, and held my arms out to her. She smiled, and in a blink of an eye, she disappeared. I cried and cried. I called my sister, Elizabeth and told her what had just occurred. We both cried. We concluded that God had given me the opportunity to see my mom again in a more positive light, so I could replace the funereal image with a Godly one.

At that moment, I realized that just because God had promised to be with me always, he didn't mean that my world would be perfect. He meant he would be there to comfort me and carry me through the hard times. That revelation caused me to look at things in a different light. From then on, I tried to look at everything as a teachable moment. When bad things happened, I tried to find God's lesson in it, realizing that though things sometimes seem bleak, there was always another day that could bring light. That became my motto and how I lived my life. Yes, there is always a better day.

CHAPTER 10

Miracle Angel Sign

Glory be to God for waking up to another day feeling like a human being again. I only have a few more days of feeling normal so I'm going to relish in it. I ordered a small chicken fryer so I'm going to be very bad and cook my favorite, fried chicken. I deserve something special. It's been far too long. My appetite is back and I'm not going to feel guilty. After all, I've lost a lot of weight so I can afford this or so I rationalized. So I whipped two eggs and placed them in a bowl. Next, I poured some flour in a zip locked bag. Then I cut a fresh lemon and squeezed juice over the chicken. I sprinkled Pappy's low sodium seasoning generously. After that, I dipped the chicken in the flour, then the egg and last the flour. I made sure I had plenty of hot oil in my new fryer to cover the chicken. I dropped the pieces of chicken into the hot oil and waited until I could see the golden brown pieces simmer. As I lifted them out, my mouth began to water. They were crispy and succulent. There's nothing better to a southern girl than fried chicken, rice, biscuits and onion gravy. I'm in paradise right now. This meal has always been my favorite since I was a child in Mississippi.

Later that night something mysterious happened. I was talking to my sister, Deloris when she mentioned the angel my neighbor had brought over as a gift. She thought that was so very nice of her. I concurred and told her I was going to turn the lights off and take a better picture of the angel and send it to her. I told her I would call her back after I had texted it to her. So I turned off all the lights downstairs which I never do until I am already upstairs every night and plugged in the angel. It was pitched black so I took a quick picture of the angel and it suddenly started radiating so brightly that it scared me. I quickly turned the lights on because that was a little scary and texted the picture to my sister. I decided to send the family a copy of the picture too. After I sent it, I looked at it more closely. I noticed something eerily scary. There was a small supernatural self-imposed figure huddled close to the angel. It appeared to have a gold halo over its bald head. The figure looked like a Buddhist priest with a long robe and white shirt under it. I could actually make out a face with distinct eyes, nose and mouth features. I was stunned! I wrote my family and asked them to examine the photo closer to see if they saw what I thought I was looking at and they saw it too! Then I knew. God was sending me another sign that he was watching over me. To me, that little figure was me and the angel was shielding me from harm. Thank you Jesus, You never change. Here you are protecting me again!

    I am filled with happiness today after seeing a sign from God yesterday. Since I can't go to church yet, I turned to Oprah's Super Soul Sunday show to get some spiritual enlightenment. Today Panache Desai, the author of "Change Your Energy, Change Your Life" was on. He talked about what is important in life. No matter what happens in life good or bad it is an act of love and grace. He uses the term, "The Divine" when he speaks of God. He says The Divine is present in all things and in all ways. A person asked him about her job and said she was unfulfilled. He answered her by saying "Our job is the excuse to which we get to love people. We are at that job or whatever because we were put in exactly the place where we needed to be to love the people that we are around." Our fulfillment comes from within and being open to allow that to happen to you. He further said that our job is an excuse to which The Divine gets to love its creations. Wow! He was so profound in his teachings. I just soak up all of his wisdom.

    Later, I thought I'd better go shopping to get some of my favorite cooking vegetables. I purchased red, yellow, green and orange bell peppers, celery, onions, yellow squash, tomatoes, mushrooms, lettuce and even a live basil plant. I felt ready for next week's cooking. Although I won't really have an appetite after chemo, these vegetables tend to give the food a better taste and they are healthy too.

    A couple of hours later, I noticed my neighbor's car was home. I thought I would go over and show her the picture of the angel she had given me and the supernatural person that showed up in the picture too. She invited me in and introduced her husband. He was working on a religious puzzle of some kind. Seeing that, made me feel that these people certainly know God. I showed them the picture. They were shocked and in awe. A God Whisper said ask her to come over to my house so that I could give her a copy of my two books. She came over and we sat down and talked and talked. I felt a real connection to my neighbor at that time. I believe God has placed her in my life for a reason. Thank you, Jesus. Oh, how I love you.

CHAPTER 11

Miracle Encounter With a Stranger

Returning to Sunnyvale Middle was wonderful. Many exciting things occurred while I was there.

I went back to graduate school to get a credential in preliminary administrative services. After teaching English for over twenty years, I became an assistant principal. I spent five years as assistant principal. I loved my job and felt I was able to help many students succeed. I was asked by the principal of Bishop Elementary School if I would consider coming over and being her assistant principal. I pondered that for a while, because I loved the students and staff at Sunnyvale Middle. But I also thought it would be a good career move, because I didn't have any elementary experience. I accepted the position and fell in love with the school right away. The staff was happy to have me there. The two secretaries and I hit it off immediately. They made life there easy, because they were so brilliant at their job. The staff grew more and more dependent on me, because the principal developed health issues and was often absent.

After that year, she decided to resign. I didn't know about it, but the entire staff sent a petition to the district's personnel office, asking them to hire me as their principal. The district was very impressed with their petition, but they still made me go through the whole interview process.

With God's help, I got the job. We were all happy. We immediately built a family atmosphere. I coined the motto, "The School Where Miracles Happen!" I knew it was God's will to place me at that school, and I believed great things were going to happen there. And they did!

Bishop went from a low performing school to a high-performing one in a single year. The teachers were extremely dedicated and worked so hard with the students after school with specially designed tutorial programs tailored to students specific learning deficiencies.. We implemented some outstanding programs before school, during and after school like Project H.E.L.P developed by Mike Goltzer and The Governor's After Schoool Program. Visiting the school were dignitaries such as Elaine Alquist, who is now a California senator; Sharon Davis, the wife of then California governor Gray Davis; and the US Secretary of Education, Richard Riley. In order to give students more access to computers, I developed a partnership with A.M.D Technology and Yahoo who donated $50,000 for a computer lab plus volunteers from their company to work with our students. The school was featured in the newspaper as one of ten schools in northern California with high English learners and poverty levels that was succeeding against the odds because our test scores were higher than schools with like socio economic populations. We received the governor's reading award six years in a row and a high-performance award from the governor. Miracles were happening all around that school. The parents, students, and teachers were so remarkable and dedicated that I felt blessed to be a part of such a positive family of educators.

After seven years at Bishop, my superintendent, Dr. Rudnicki, asked me to return to Sunnyvale Middle and become principal because the principal who had been there for over thirty years was retiring. My superintendent was a wonderful manager. He gave me the opportunity to put my vision for Bishop in place. He never micro-managed and believed in my abilities. We spent many hours discussing my vision for Bishop. I loved the way he questioned me and made me reflect strategically on exactly why I wanted to do certain programs. With his guidance, I became a better principal. Therefore, when he asked me to consider going back to Sunnyvale Middle, I told him I'd think about it. In the back of mind, I was thinking there was no way I was leaving Bishop! Everyone was so phenomenal! Why would I leave there?

I had purchased a home in Tracy, which was sixty miles from Sunnyvale. It took me ninety minutes to get to work on the train or by car. I didn't care, because God had managed to help me get a beautiful home for far less money than the ones in Sunnyvale. One particular morning, I boarded the train. My usual routine was to close my eyes for thirty minutes just to relax, because I had to get up at five o'clock to catch the train by six. Then I would check my e-mails and work on projects and memos for school. But this particular morning, as I sat comfortably in my seat with my eyes closed, a stranger sat opposite me. This train had some seats that faced each other with a small table between. Well, this stranger sat down and I, of course, looked up for a moment, expecting to close my eyes again to get some needed rest. My eyes, however, caught a glimpse of two Bibles she had placed on the table in front of me. Puzzled, I thought, *That's strange. Why does she need two Bibles? Oh well, that's not my business.* So I closed my eyes. Suddenly, this woman burst into my peace and said ever so gently, "Oh, is this your book?" It was a red calendar I always carried with me. I bought one for each of the teachers as back to school gifts. On the cover were the school's name and address. She proceeded to invade my space. "Oh, are you a teacher?"

"No, I'm the principal, but like I always say, once a teacher always a teacher," I replied. We both smiled, breaking the ice.

Then she said, "You enjoy your work, don't you? I can tell in your voice that you enjoy your work." She looked intently in my eyes, as if she were looking into my very soul. For some strange reason, I started telling this stranger about all the programs we were doing at Bishop and how proud I was of the staff and students. I rambled on about all the miracles we were blessed with and couldn't stop bragging. She smiled broadly and said, "Looks like you've done great work there!" I smiled too and told her my superintendent had asked me if I wanted to leave and go back to my previous school. Laughing, I told her I wasn't considering that, because I was happy with Bishop. She looked more intently, and her voice sounded like a mother talking to a child. She said, "Maybe he wants you to spread some of that positive energy to another group of teachers, like you did at Bishop. Have you thought that maybe you've done as much as you need to do at Bishop, and it's time to move on and take your gift somewhere else."

"Why should I give up what I have at Bishop for something totally new?"

"Because it's time!" The conductor called out for a stop, and the stranger got up and walked off into the distance. Her words echoed in my head. It reminded me of my talk with God, especially when she said, "Because it's time."

I was shaken by the conversation. When I returned to school the next day, I talked it over with my assistant principal, Eric Panosian. He wasn't hearing any of what I had to say, so I spoke to my secretaries Hilda and Carol. They, too, disregarded my conversation about leaving because they did not want me to even think about leaving them.

Every morning, I looked for the woman on the train, but she didn't show up. This went on for about a week. Then it happened. I was getting out of my car when I heard yelling. I looked around, and there she was, walking rather briskly to the train. She hollered to me, "Have you thought about what we talked about? Do it. It's God's will!"

Fumbling, I got out of the car determined to catch up with this stranger and delve more into this, but by the time I got to the train, she had disappeared. I walked to the next car through and through and could not find the stranger. I sat down in disbelief. Had I encountered an angel? I felt like God was speaking to me and wanted me to make the move—even though I didn't want to.

That night, I prayed on it and felt a sense of relief as I made my decision to leave Bishop. I went to Dr. Rudnicki and told him of my decision to take the position at Sunnyvale Middle. I knew it was meant to be, because he said he was going to appoint me to the school rather than have me go through the interview process. He said he had complete faith in my abilities to bring positive energy and leadership to the school. I called a staff meeting at Bishop and told them about my encounter with the stranger. By then they knew how spiritual I was and how I believed in miracles. They couldn't argue with me, so they just filed by one by one and hugged me, crying. I promised them I would leave them in good hands, and Eric Panosian became principal. I felt a sense of relief, because I knew he would keep Bishop's vision going.

My first staff meeting at Sunnyvale Middle was great. I shared my story of the stranger with them, too. Some were believers, but some were not, so I knew I had my work cut out with them. I didn't worry though. I knew I'd win them over. Sunnyvale Middle School was where I was supposed to be. It was where I started and where I was going to end my educational career: a real full circle. At Sunnyvale, I coined the motto "Dream it, Believe it, Achieve it!" We really made that motto a reality. Our vision for the school became a reality. The staff, students, and parents were a joy to be around. A few of the teachers were still there from when I was a teacher at Sunnyvale Middle. They made things a lot easier and spoke to teachers about my success as a teacher when I served with them. I enjoyed my work with my assistant principals. We worked closely to implement changes and a positive environment. We had many noteworthy programs and acquired many rewards at Sunnyvale Middle. When I retired in 2009, we had exceeded our goal for the California Stars Test and gone from 785 to 825. Usually schools were able to reach between 3 or 4 points from one year to the next. We exceeded the state's expectation by twenty-five points. We were on our way to greatness, and I knew I could retire in peace. After thirty-nine years in education, I was ready for my next phase.

God still has plans for me, and I am waiting with bated breath for my next journey.

"Here I am! I stand at the door and knock.
If you hear my voice and open the door,
I will come in."

Revelation 3:20

CHAPTER 12

Phoenix Rising from the Ashes

1 Corinthian: 3:15 "If any man's work shall be burned, he shall suffer loss: but he himself shall be saved; yet so as through fire."

It was a warm sunny Sunday morning on May 22, 2022, as I sleepily awoke, putting on my robe, gathering my glasses, cell phone and heading downstairs. As with my morning ritual, I took my morning medication with probiotics and Vitamin D3 and made my Pike's Peak Starbucks coffee.

I settled down into my comfortable lounge chair and pulled out my morning devotional, **Jesus Calling**. As I turned to May 22 the words cried out to me. "When things do not go as you would like, accept the situation immediately. If you indulge in feelings of regret, they can easily spill over the line into resentment. I am sovereign over your circumstances and humble yourself under my mighty hand. Rejoice in what I am doing in your life, even though it is beyond your understanding."

Sipping my warm cup of coffee, I reflected on those words. Sometimes I want God to intervene and answer my prayers right away. Being human, I lose patience and want to do my own will, however this Bible verse helped to put that into perspective. I needed to realize that God knows what I am going through, so I just need to have more faith and put it in his hands and wait for him to take care of the situation. After contemplating the devotional reading, I picked up my phone to tune in to the morning church service which was done remotely ever since the dreaded covid occurred. I did not like the remote service as much as sitting in the sanctuary with other believers. The clapping, singing spiritual hymns and hearing people shout amen just stirred my soul more. However, it was the best I could do under the circumstances.

Settling into my recliner with my Bible in hand and phone, I turned to the video of my church service. The organ, drums and guitarists were playing my favorite songs, and it stirred my soul. Afterwards, the pastor started preaching. Suddenly, my sense of smell alerted me that something was burning. I sniffed and sniffed and was assured that the smell was real. I suddenly got up and went into the kitchen to see if there was anything on the stove although I knew I was not cooking anything. I looked around and there was nothing burning. Okay I thought to myself, my mind is playing tricks on me. I settled back into the chair to resume listening to the sermon, but my nose kept smelling something. I thought to myself, it is outside because sometimes the fire department burns grass on the Altamont Pass as a preventative. I got up and went out front and I could smell a scent of burning in the air. Okay I thought that is what it was all along.

Just as I sat down in my recliner, I heard this loud pop, pop, pop sound. I jumped up and ran straight to the back door. As I opened the back patio door, I saw this raging fire along the back fence and the bottom of the wooden patio deck. My heart was racing. My reaction was mixed as to what to do. I picked up the garden hose, but the darn sprayer was broken, and no water was coming out. I thought I could get a bucket of water but when I looked up, the fire was moving too fast. Frantic, thinking the fire was spreading too fast, I ran upstairs to wake up my grandson who was sleeping. We were both scared out of our minds. I grabbed my purse and cell phone and told my grandson to move his car. I managed to dial 911 but my fingers were shaking, and I could barely dial the numbers. Next, I quickly ran to the neighbors to warn them of the fire, but they were not home. I moved my car down the streets so the firefighters could get to the house. I was so bewildered and frightened.

I sat on the sidewalk stoop across from the house as the fire trucks arrived. I counted a lot of them. They were racing into the house and around the back. I saw water shooting up all over the house. I felt like I was having an out of body experience. People were driving by to see what was happening, neighbors were pouring out of their homes, people on the side streets were running down to the corner where my house was, and it was a total nightmare. One neighbor brought me a chair to sit in and I was touched by his gesture. I managed to finally realize that I needed to call my son who lived in San Jose. He was shocked and said he was on his way. What a great son!

The captain of the fire department came over. He knelt beside me to ask what had happened. He took notes. His voice was very calm, and he asked me if I was insured. I told him I was. He said the fire was out and that they were able to save the house.

He also said that Tracy only had seven fire stations and luckily for me five of them were able to come to save my house. This was indeed a miracle that there were no other fires at that time. I was so grateful and thanked him profusely. He said that if I wanted him too, he could take me into the house to get the policy because the windows needed to be boarded up for the night. When I walked into the house, I was in total disbelief. Everything was black from the smoke. Ashes were all over the floor and furniture. Water was soaking the floor, and the windows were shattering.

As the firefighter led me up the blackened stairs, I was bewildered but I managed to find my insurance papers and head back downstairs. We went back outside, and I fumbled through the papers trying to find the phone number but could not find it. The kind firefighter asked if he could help, and I said yes right away. My neighbor ran to her house and brought me a pen and pad to write things down. The firefighter found the phone number and I called. Because it was Sunday, there was only a call center receptionist. She was only going to take down the information and relay it for Monday, but the firefighter asked for the phone. He let them know that he was the Fire captain and that they needed to send out a company to board up six windows to secure the property and make sure I was safe. Sure enough, someone was sent out to board up all the windows. He snatched down all the blinds and covered every window with boards. I thank God for this firefighter. He was a lifesaver. I knew nothing about dealing with insurance companies. I had paid for over 20 years but never had to deal with them. This was the beginning of a yearlong process. I am going to take you on this journey with me because there are things, I learned which may help you if you ever find yourself in a comparable situation. The yearlong journey will also show you just how God was with me every step of the way.

My son, Charles, arrived just in time as the firefighters were leaving. Charles, who is a banker, is my levelheaded calm son. He had just jumped in his car and drove from San Jose to Tracy as soon as I called him. Charles, my grandson, and I went back into the house. We were all shaken by the appearance of the house. We slowly went to look at the back of the house. The fence, overhead trellis or pagoda and wooden patio were burned to the ground. To my surprise, the wooden shed was nowhere to be found. It was totally burned. There were big pipes all over the ground. Later I learned, the silver pipes came out of the fireplace. Charles took videos of the burned areas and sent them to the family so they could see the devastation. As I entered back into the house, I noticed that holes were cut into the sheet rock on both sides of the fireplace. The walls were all black with smoke and the house smelled of smoke. The firefighter had said that I would not be able to stay in the house that night, so my son and I discussed what to do next. He offered to take me to San Jose to his home, but I knew that I would be too far away to take care of the house situation. We decided to look for nearby hotels. I got out my AARP hotel card and he looked at his Hilton card and other hotels. We settled at Microtel not too far from the house. It looked fine and it was not too expensive.

My grandson, Royale and I stayed there about a week. My grandson is a terrible snorer. It sounded like a big rig truck in that room. He had his bed next to mine. I wanted to throw a pillow across the room in the middle of the night. After contacting the insurance adjuster, he assured me that he would meet with me in a couple of days to assess the damage. Along with him was the Restoration Clean up Associate, Tawnya and crew. We all met at the burned house. The insurance adjustor had his person take pictures inside every room and outside where the fire started. He went from room to room and took copious notes. Finally, he said he was finished and would submit the report to his boss.

He then left and I was able to talk more with the Restoration Clean up person. As we chatted about small talk, I mentioned that my grandson was driving me crazy sleeping next to me in the hotel room. She said that was not a good situation for me and I should not have dealt with that. He had his own room at my house. According to my insurance policy, however many rooms or whatever you were accustomed to at your old house, you can have similar accommodations in your rental space. She also informed me of a recently new hotel nearby. As miracles would have it, I was able to get two large spacious rooms for me and my grandson. It was lovely with breakfast free and a beautiful pool as well. I was thankful to God for sending me someone like her.

What did I need a Restoration Clean Up person for I wondered. Well, I soon found out. The Restoration Clean Up Company is responsible for Smoke, Water and Mold damage as well as Contents. They brought in a big machine which blew air into the walls to prevent mold damage and it stayed on for two whole days. They sent in a cleaning crew who cleaned the kitchen stove, refrigerator, counters, and cabinets. They even cleaned my granddaughters' toys in the garage and organized the entire garage. They threw out unsalvageable things and labeled them as such. An entire crew came out and took every piece of furniture and every stitch of clothing out of every drawer and closet in my house. Unfortunately, I was not home when this was done. I was at the hotel. When I went back to the house, I was shocked to find everything had been boxed up and taken away. I did not have enough clothes or underwear with me at the hotel. I thought of buying new clothes but instead I frantically called Tawnya to ask why I was not informed about the day the pack out as they call it was happening. I was told they were going to remove everything, but she forgot to tell me which date. She apologized profusely and asked what clothes I needed. I had just ordered a ton of Caftans for the summer, so I asked her to look in the master bedroom closet and bring about eight of them. The very next morning, I heard a knock on the door and when I opened it to my surprise there was a hanger full of pressed caftans!

A genuinely nice lady named April called from the fire department. She wanted to know how things were going. I explained about concerns I had. First, the back fence was burned down to the ground, and neighbors were walking by taking pictures and looking at the burned house and me. She assured me that a temporary fence needed to be put up for safety purposes. She called a company and had them come out right away. I was sure God had placed another angel in my life. Every time something concerned me, April was right there to help. When the contractors wanted to put the old blackened dirty blinds back up, she intervened on my behalf and got them written off. She even contacted the blinds people to help speed up the process of getting them in every room in the house. She was an expert on fire situations. I was so fortunate to have her.

We stayed at that hotel for two weeks before I received a phone call from a lady who said she was with Renewal Claims Solution. My insurance adjustor had called her and asked her to call me to inform me that paying for two rooms at the hotel was expensive. It looked like it was going to take more than two weeks to get things back in order at the house. If fact, it might take two or three months. To my dismay, that was a real shock. She said we needed to look at rental houses or Air BnB's. Overnight, it occurred to me that I did not want to rent another person's house but would rather rent my own apartment. I called Lisa, the Renewal person and explained that to her. She said she would get on that right away. Just a couple of days later, she called to say she had found a new apartment complex called the Harvest Apartments happened to have an opening of a three-bedroom apartment. The lease was for three months but I had to hurry and go over to see if I liked it before it was snatched up. I had not heard of this new apartment complex but was eager to see it, so I went down to look at it.

Lisa called Jeremy, the manager, and told him I was on my way, and I would meet him there. He gave me the royal tour. It was spectacular. The grounds had majestic palm trees, meticulously trimmed hedges, resident community gardens, a huge swimming pool, a spacious gym and even a basketball court. He then drove me over to my apartment building. It looked like a beautiful townhouse with three large bedrooms upstairs. The master bedroom was larger than mine at home with a huge sunken separate tub and an accommodating shower. Downstairs, the kitchen had all stainless-steel appliances, laminate flooring, and soft plush carpet on the stairs. I was blown away and I could not sign that lease fast enough. My goodness, this was a miraculous find. Then to my surprise, Lisa explained that when I moved in, she would have a furniture company bring furniture to completely furnish the place.

We moved in and the same day the furniture arrived. It was like Christmas. All the furniture was white. The couch was white; the long stately dining room table was brown, but the elegant chairs were all white. Every bed linen and even the bedspread was white. Every towel was white as well. Wow, I thought, I must keep this place spotless. I ordered plastic covers for the chairs and couch because my six-year-old granddaughter was coming to visit for the summer and my four-year-old granddaughter and my son Trevis, and his wife from North Carolina were coming to visit as well. It had been planned before the fire so luckily, I had somewhere for them to stay. God again was sure looking out for me. Blessings were happening.

Meanwhile, I was visiting the house every day. I did not stop the mail from coming so I was checking the mail and receiving Amazon and Fed Ex packages nearly every day.

Dealing with the insurance adjustor and the A2Z Contractors was a nightmare. At first, the contractors had to submit estimates on costs to the insurance adjustor. Then it would take forever for the two of them to settle on the cost. I did not know that I would be responsible for paying all of the vendors. First, vendors had to submit their costs to the insurance company who agreed to the estimates given to them. After the service was rendered, I had to write a check to them. It was all a process which at first left my head spinning but then I remembered that I was a principal before I retired and had renovated two schools. I decided to put on my principal's hat again and take care of this situation. I had to go online and fill out paperwork with my bank. Because my bank was a lienholder, every check had to be signed by both of us. The bank had a step-by-step process. All contractors estimate documents had to be uploaded. Then once it was verified, I had to submit the checks from the insurance company. The banks held one third of the money until they sent out an inspector to assure that the work was 50% done as submitted. The rest of the money was to be released when the work was finished. It took a while to get everything uploaded to the bank's website. Patience is a virtue in this case. I took a picture of every check just in case. I opened a separate checking account with a credit card and check book to deposit only insurance money. I knew I had to pay out vendors and did not want to mix my personal money with the insurance money. I bought a large accordion type of folder to place all brochures from vendors, insurance papers, and receipts for anything dealing with the house. I got every business card from vendors, their receptionist or boss. I needed to be super organized and ready for this situation and believe me I needed all of this. There were so many times, I had to call or reinforce or clarify that something was paid or that the insurance company had not paid me yet. Keeping good records was the key to my sanity.

Some exciting things happened along the way and some not so exciting, but I will recall a few for you. My carpet was old and blackened from soot and smoke. The insurance company said it was ruined so I had a choice of a new carpet. The bedrooms and dining room also had black smoke in the carpet. The carpet cleaning company said they could not clean it to look like it was before the fire, so it all had to be removed and replaced. What a blessing!

Luckily, I had my thinking cap on, and I asked if I could replace it with laminate flooring which is what I had been dreaming of for a while. To my amazement, the insurance adjustor said that if the amount is comparable to the amount allowed for that item, then it could be done. I asked the contractor to get me an estimate of the carpet and laminate and compare costs. He did and we were able to find laminate for similar pricing. We had a problem with my fireplace too. The City of Tracy no longer allowed old fireplaces to be rebuilt so they said either get rid of the fireplace or get an electric or gas fireplace instead. It took some work because my fireplace was on the opposite side of where the power was. At first, they said it could not be done but miraculously they found a way to encase a wire all around the house to the other side and it worked beautifully. I now have a gorgeous fireplace which lights up in ten different flames. The wood and embers all change colors too. It is a real beauty. The other problem dealt with the insurance company only wanting to rebuild half the patio deck, half the pagoda or trellis and half the fence because only half of those things burned. It took a lot of praying and fighting over that. Finally, the City of Tracy came out and said the wooden patio deck was never built to code. It was sitting on dirt and could not be rebuilt that way. Also, the pagoda would not be safe if only part of it was done to code so both the patio and pagoda had to be replaced. I was so happy that the Lord had answered my prayers. That took months to be approved by the insurance company and the City.

Realizing, this building situation was going to take more than three months, the insurance company said I had only one month before the allowance for the apartment would run out of money and based on the insurance quota if my house was "habitable" I could move back in. I had to get the contractors on the ball and get the house painted on the inside, carpet put in and laminate flooring done in a month I came over to the house everyday with my granddaughter and called them every day. I kept a calendar of when they said they would be out doing certain jobs and if they did not show up, I called their boss. The painter did not show up for several days and when I called his boss, they said he had covid. So, I gave him a few days break to recover and then got on them again. I called my friend, April, to tell her I was moving back home but because of my bad back, I did not know how I was going to clean the house. It was all dirty and dusty after three months. Sure enough, April came through. She said the insurance company would send the cleaning crew back out to clean again before I moved back in, and they did. Getting all the furniture put back in was a chore. I finally called April who told me about pack back. This is when the Restoration Clean Up Company brings back your furniture, electronics and puts everything back and you just tell them where it should go. What a lifesaver that was! I am sure God put April in my life. The things I knew nothing about April enlightened me. Surely, she was sent by God. Things were coming together finally. The inside of the house looked beautiful with freshly painted walls, new carpet and laminate flooring and pristine furniture. I could breathe a sigh of relief. I was back home again, and I would be able to be there to supervise the repairs of the outside of the house.

The outside of the house took many twists and turns. The rains in California set everything back for months. It took much prayer and pressure to get the entire fence rebuilt but it finally came together. It was remarkable to see a new redwood fence stretched across my backyard. Above the fence, I could see the white billowing cumulus clouds and iridescent sunsets. I decided on stamped concrete instead of the old wood patio from before and the tinted stained redwood deck blended beautifully with the redwood fence. The white pagoda extended across the patio deck and looked amazing. The backyard was a sight to behold. I look back over the year and I can see God's handiwork all around. I feel like a Phoenix rising from the ashes.

I am reminded of the bible verse of Isaiah 43:2 "When you pass through the waters, I will be with you; and through the rivers, they shall not overwhelm you; when you walk through fire you shall not be burned, and the flame shall not consume you."

CHAPTER 13

I Heard the Voice of God

"You can't leave me!" Charles exploded. "You are nothing without me!" Usually, I would let this insult to my abilities stand, and my self-esteem was at such a low state I had actually believed him. But no more. I was stronger and more determined than ever that enough was enough. Once before, I had threatened to leave and had actually packed a few suitcases. Charles became very erratic and started screaming the luggage was his because he had purchased it for a family trip to Jamaica. He started screaming that it was his luggage, and I should put it down. That day I weaseled out and stayed on. This day, however, I ran to the kitchen and grabbed some large garbage bags. I went to the children's room and emptied their dresser drawers into the bags. Then I proceeded to my closet, pulled down tons of clothes, and tossed them and their hangers into the bag. Charles followed me, screaming at me the entire time. I was scared, but I was not going to be swayed this time. Charles cornered me with fire in his eyes. "Give me my ring back," he screamed. I gave him all the rings on my hand, including the wedding band, to avoid confrontation. He yelled, "Give me my necklace." I gave him my gold necklace, which he had bought me as an anniversary present. I willingly gave him everything, because I knew it was a tactic to break my spirit.

Finally, he screamed, "Give me the car keys." That's when I snapped into action. No, he was not getting those keys. I ran to the boys and grabbed Desmond's and Trevis's hands. I took them to the front door, ran upstairs to get the clothes I had packed and threw down the garbage bags. Charles screamed at the boys. "Come back here. Don't go with your mother. She can't take care of you. You are going to be homeless, sleeping in cars." The boys were crying and I ushered them to the car, telling them all the while that it was going to be all right. Their little eyes looked so frightened. I felt so sorry that my boys had to witness such a painful event. Shaking, I got behind the wheel. I was so scared; all I could think of was safety. Thank God we got out safely, without Charles getting violent.

 As I drove away, I started thinking about where we could go. I had girlfriends but I didn't want to impose on them. Then it came to me. There was a hotel a few blocks from the house. I could go there for at least a day to calm my nerves and get the boys settled. When I checked into the hotel, I had enough money for the one night with a little left over. The only reason I had that cash was because Charles and I put both our checks together to pay for the bills. We both kept out enough for lunch and small necessities. Charles managed the bills, so I didn't know much about the finances. Unfortunately, all of the credit cards were in his name. I knew I would get paid at the end of the month, but at that moment, I had nothing except that little bit of cash. How was I going to take care of my precious boys? Silently I prayed for God's help. Trying to keep up a brave face, I took the boys downstairs and bought them sodas and chips, which calmed them a little. Out of the blue, I thought about the new apartments I had seen near the house. It was a long shot, but I decided to see if there were any apartments available. I told Lil Charles what I was going to do and told him to watch his brothers until I got back. At fifteen, he was such a brave, dependable, young man.

 I drove to the new apartments and asked to speak with the manager. I stammered and poured out my whole story to this complete stranger. I told her I had just left my husband, who was mentally abusive, and had taken my boys to a hotel. I admitted I only had enough cash for one night at the hotel. I really needed a place to stay. I assured her I had a good job as a teacher and could pay her at the end of the month. When I finished, she said she was very sympathetic, but they didn't have any apartments available. She asked me for my information in case something became available later, so I filled out the form and left. Crushed, I sat in the car, thinking about what to do. I didn't want to call my family, because they were all the way in Mississippi and would be worried. I sat there for a while and prayed to God for wisdom and strength. Suddenly, I felt a serenity come over me. I knew God was going to answer my prayers somehow. With a brave soul, I went back to the hotel, hugged my boys, and told them everything was going to be fine. Because they had always trusted me, they trusted me at that moment. I thanked God again.

The next day, I took the boys to school and went straight to work. It was difficult to concentrate, but I put on a brave face and took care of my students. A few hours later, I received a phone call from the office, saying there was a phone message waiting for me. I was hoping it wasn't from Charles, because I really didn't want to talk to him. When my preparation time came, I went to the office and picked up the message. To my surprise, it was from the apartment manager. "Hello," I said, "this is Frances Dampier."

She said, "Frances, I thought about what you told me all last night and couldn't get you out of my mind. Something told me I needed to help you and your boys. If I can't help another woman get out of an abusive relationship, what kind of woman am I. Listen, I want you to come by today and pick up your keys. You can move in tonight if you like. Luckily, I have a two-bedroom apartment that just became available, and we just refurbished it. There are other people on the waiting list, but you impressed me so much that I moved you up to the top of the list. Oh, I will waive the move-in fees, and your first payment will be due the first of next month." I blurted out about three thank-yous. Jesus, Jesus, this had to be you! He had answered my call. This had to be a miracle.

As soon as school was over, I ran out the door and right over to the apartment. I prayed the whole way over, "Please don't let her change her mind!" When I arrived, she greeted me so graciously. We reviewed the contract, and she gave me the keys. I squeezed those keys so tightly, I'm sure they left an imprint in my hands. Grateful, I thanked her profusely and drove off to pick up the boys. Gleefully, I told them we had a new apartment and were moving in that night. Lil Charles reminded me we didn't have any furniture. Suddenly an idea hit me. Charles taught a few nights a week, and this particular night he was not going to be home until around ten o'clock. We decided to go back to the house and get the mattresses from the bunk beds. While there, the boys gathered some of their favorite things and their schoolbooks. I grabbed some food from the refrigerator. Lil Charles and I tied the mattresses on top of the car.

We felt better as we left and hurried to our new place. The boys liked it a lot. It was not far from our house, so the neighborhood was familiar. We put the mattresses together on the floor, took a walk around the apartment complex and came back so the boys could complete their homework. The boys were a little giddy about the swimming pool; they couldn't wait to get in. At least something had gotten their minds off the horrible situation, and things were looking up for us. After homework, we settled in for a good night's sleep on our mattresses. We prayed as usual, and I assured them everything was going to be fine.

That premonition came true that very night. I can remember it as if it happened yesterday, but it was not yesterday: it was the spring of 1987. I cannot do justice to what I am about to describe. I do not have adequate words to relate to you the sacred vision that took place that night. I've struggled with ways to make it believable, but I've just decided to write it out in script format. This is what happened.

GOD: "Frances, Frances!"

I woke up, startled, and looked around the room. From the light of the clock, I could see the boys beside me, sound asleep. I looked again at the alarm clock. It read one o'clock. Shaken and frightened, I scanned the room, but it was pitched dark. Suddenly, I heard my name again.

GOD: "Frances!"

I sat straight up. *I really am hearing this,* I thought. *Someone is calling my name. What in God's name? Who is calling me?* My heart pounded.

GOD: "Don't be afraid. I am here!"

Although I had never heard God's voice before, I knew instantly that he was there with me. My heart stood still. I was not fearful anymore. In fact, I felt a peaceful sensation. Through some sort of telepathy, I blurted nonverbally, *Oh God, where have you been? I've been calling for you to help me with this marriage for years, and now I have left Charles. I have these three boys to take care of, and I don't know what to do!*

GOD: "My child, I have been with you every step of the way."

As soon as he finished speaking, he flashed a living scene before my eyes. I was watching Charles and I arguing over something mean he had said to me, and I saw myself running into the bedroom, crying. I saw myself asking God for help. Then, in a split second, another scene appeared, showing me the next day. I was coming home late after the funeral of a sorority sister's husband. He had died young of a brain tumor. I had taken a Pyrex dish of macaroni and cheese to serve the guests after the funeral services. Trying to juggle my keys and the dish caused me to lose my balance, and the Pyrex dish flew into the air and bounced on the concrete steps. It came down and sliced my leg wide open. I felt a trickle down my leg, and when I looked down, I saw my leg lay wide open; you could see the meaty white portion and the glass had cut to the bone. I screamed for Charles, and when he saw my leg, he gathered the boys and hurried to the hospital. They had to perform surgery. It took them a while, because they had to put in over one hundred stitches. The doctor said I would probably have nerve damage, because the glass had severed several nerves. Instead of being supportive, Charles was irritated and kept asking when we could go, because he had to work the next day. I saw myself sitting there in the hospital bed, looking sad and dejected. God's voice jolted me back to reality. His voice was intense, strong, and powerful.

GOD: "That was not the time!"

Then, in a flash, another scene appeared before my eyes. I saw myself at home after work. The phone rang, and I went over to answer it. It was Charles's sister-in-law, screaming that his brother had died of a massive heart attack. In his thirties, he was too young to die. I was visibly shaken but calmed myself long enough to call Charles to get him home. Charles was distraught, and who could blame him? He became withdrawn and didn't want to talk or be consoled. So his brother's wife and I took care of the funeral arrangements and had his body shipped back to Mississippi, as his mother and family requested. We all flew back with his body for the funeral and burial. Charles was so hurt, but he held everything in, trying not to show any emotion. He pushed everyone away, and even when the boys tried to comfort him, he turned away from them. I felt sorry for him, and though I tried my hardest to comfort him, he showed no indication he cared what I thought. I saw myself with tears in my eyes, sitting in the church pews, feeling sad and dejected and in need of God's help. I heard God's voice jolt me back to reality.

GOD: "That was not the time!"

A third scene flashed before my eyes. I watched myself get up and go to the telephone. The voice on the line was that of the woman, who had called me to tell me of the affair she had been having with my husband. It had been ten long years since that terrible incident. A sickening feeling came to the pit of my stomach. God showed me how difficult it had been for me to weather that storm. I saw myself in the bathroom, hiding from the children, so they could not see me crying in pain. There in my solitude, down on my knees, I prayed to God for help. I saw myself clutching my chest, thinking I was going to die but knowing I was only having anxiety attacks. God showed me going into the medicine cabinet and taking more and more aspirin to calm my aching head. Somehow, my thoughts were being read. I was thinking that I wasn't going to live through this marriage, and my children were going to be without a mother. I was thinking, *God help me before this marriage kills me*. The scene revealed how after praying, I felt a sense of strength, as if God had heard my prayers and given me the willpower to get out of the marriage. As I picked myself up from the floor, I felt empowered and determined that I could leave. This time, I didn't feel sad and dejected. I smiled and got ready to face Charles. Suddenly, God's voice echoed these four words three times:

GOD: "Now is the time! Now is the time! Now is the time!" I was speechless. I fell to my knees and prayed furiously.

ME: "Oh, God, thank you heavenly father. I am sorry for ever doubting you and your love for me.

Father forgive me for doubting you, and forgive me for every wrong I have ever done."

At that moment, a flood of all the not so good things I had ever done flashed before my eyes. I saw the smallest things, like taking a lollipop from the store, to stealing my friend's boyfriend. The worst one was seeing my mother cry over the relationship I was having with an older man. She thought he was going to keep me from getting a good college education. God seemed to linger longer on that scene. I think he was upset with me for hurting my mother, because I suddenly heard this loud echo three times.

GOD: "It will never be! It will never be! It will never be!"

Well, I figured God was telling me that relationship was not going to happen. At that very moment, every little bit of feeling I had for that guy was completely washed away, as if it was never there. I knew in an instant that God had washed away all of my sins. I felt a warm sensation from head to foot, as if my body was being cleansed. Suddenly, I heard God's voice again, but this time it was more gentle and soft. It actually gave me a peace and complete serenity.

GOD: "Don't worry about anything. All you have to do is trust in me and listen to my word. I will be with you always, always, always.

His voice drifted away, echoing ever so softly. Tears streaming down my face, I lay back down, replaying the vision over and over in my tiny little brain, trying to comprehend what I had witnessed. Did I just have a conversation with God? What would people say? I didn't care at that moment. I soon drifted off to a peaceful sleep, feeling all warm and cuddly and knowing I was in God's hands.

When the alarm went off in the morning, I woke up feeling like I had been given an elixir. Euphoria enveloped my body. It was as if I was being lifted from the ground. My feet were touching the ground, but my body felt like it was floating. My entire body was transformed into this new being. I felt like a heavy weight had been ripped from my body. It was such an incredible joy that no words can give it justice. When I got to school, I was beaming. People asked me why I was so happy. I told two people. One happened to be a Christian I presumed, and he believed me right away. He was fascinated with my revelation. The other teacher was doubtful and kept trying to deflate my enthusiasm. She kept telling me it must have been a dream. I realized at that moment that this was something I couldn't share with just anyone, because usually the only people who said they heard the voice of God were lunatics. I decided to keep this to myself, because I didn't want to destroy my joy and the precious sacred gift.

CHAPTER 14

Paris Trip Vision Revealed

At last, forty years later I finally embarked on my trip to Paris, a dream of a lifetime. I took French in high school and college anticipating a trip to Paris in the near future, but as life, marriage, career, and children would have it, the dream of Paris was placed on the backburner. Now, after retirement, the dream was finally realized. The all-inclusive eight-day cruise was going to be unbelievable. A tour guide was given the task of escorting us on a daily excursion to the city of Paris and surrounding notable areas. It was a miraculous adventure witnessing the Champs-Élysées and the glorious sights along the Seine River. Along this boulevard was the world capital of exquisite shopping! The finest luxury designer brands lined the street with famous stores like Chanel, Dior, and Azzaro. This was a fashionista's dream.

Drifting along the Seine on our ship, we were able to view the sheer beauty of monuments indicative of the Industrial Age, all stately standing in glory, such as the Petit Palais, the Grand Palais, the Eiffel Tower, the Notre Dame Cathedral, the Conciergerie, and the gigantic palace of the Louvre. Strolling down the streets of Paris smelling and tasting the mouthwatering buttery croissants with hot ham and cheese oozing out of it, dribbling down the corners of my mouth and later biting into the warm, sweet, flaky crepes made me realize that all was right with the world.

Visiting historical sites like Auvers-sur-Oise where Van Gogh painted over fifty masterpieces and later died of alcoholism and manic depression, gave me insight into some of his most famous work. Exciting as well was visiting the city of Rouen, where breathtaking cathedrals displayed master craftsmanship of biblical images and carvings on the wall and windows. This city was also famous for being the place where Joan of Arc was burned at the stake for expressing that she had heard a "God Whisper" telling her to take back France from England. Because she had faith and listened to God, people called her a witch and burned her at the stake. Seeing her gravesite and statue was a testimony of her strong belief in God. Doing God's will is not always easy. Another memorable sight was seeing the D-Day beaches, museum, and memorial for the 9,000 soldiers still buried there. This sight, with an array of white crosses with a backdrop of soldiers' names inscribed along the walls, caused my heart to stand still and I became awestruck, inspired, and extremely grateful for their great service to our country.

Thinking God had given me the miracle of a lifetime with my Paris trip made my heart sing praises, but to my amazement that was not the reason for my trip to Paris. God had something else entirely different in mind for me, a commandment/mission that left me speechless and awe-inspired.

It all began when our tour guide asked us if we wanted her to show us how to use the Metro, Paris' train. Three new friends that I had formed a close bond with on the tour and I quickly raised our hands along with some other people. We had seen earlier on the tour bus an entire street of flea markets with souvenir shops and all kinds of delicious tasty foods. We couldn't wait to get there. Taking the train was scary, so I wrote meticulous notes while the guide told us which streets to look for and which transfer to take to get to the flea market. We spent the day shopping, eating, laughing, trying on berets and literally just enjoying the day until suddenly it started pouring rain. Immediately, we ran back to the metro station. Soaking wet and cold, I pulled out my wet directions on how to navigate our way back through the train maze and figure out the transfer back to the ship. As we were walking through the Metro, two other people, Laura and Katlyn, who looked very lost, from our Viking tour were also trying to figure their way out of the maze. Although we had never officially met, we noticed their Viking badges right away; therefore, we joined forces, determined that we would figure it out together. One of them, Laura seemed drawn to me right away, and as we walked and searched for the next street sign, she instantly began telling me that she was so happy to be in Paris and that she just had to make the journey to Paris because her doctor had given her only six months to live. She had been diagnosed with pancreatic cancer and she was searching for answers. Startled by her admission, I blurted out that I believed in miracles. I didn't want to give her false hope, so I continued by saying that God would show her the direction to take and that he would guide her no matter what the outcome. I told her to trust in God and listen for answers from the Holy Spirit. That day we bonded and became friends throughout the trip. Laura, Katlyn, Ethel, and their husbands, Jonathan, Sal, and Derrick, plus Denise and her mother began eating together every night and bonding on our various tour trips. We talked about everything and had so many wonderful laughs. We found out that Katlyn and Sam were going to get married on the ship and we all put our heads together to help plan it and make it a joyous occasion. What fun we were having!

After one of our delicious dinners, I went seeking the program director, Sam. I asked him if he could find out where the Lady of Lourdes' city was because I knew it was in France. I informed him that six or seven of us wanted to take a side trip there. I also told him that I had met this beautiful young lady who said she only had six months to live and I knew people took pilgrimages to the city of Lourdes because the water was said to have miraculous powers and could cure illnesses. The program director, Sam, researched and finally told me that we couldn't go there because it was five hundred miles away. I blurted out to Sam, "I don't understand why God put this idea in my head. I thought this was going to be a miracle for Laura." Sam looked up at me and uttered with certainty, "I don't believe in miracles!" My eyes widened, and without thinking, I said, "What? Well, Sam, just wait until the end of the week. God's going to show you some miracles. Mark my word." Why I said that, I don't have a clue, and I was puzzled myself as to why I even thought of the city of Lourdes. Usually, I consider those thoughts to be associated with "God Whispers."

After the most fabulous three-course meal, I decided to turn in for the night. Settling into a relaxing slumber, with the waves crashing against the ship and rocking me ever so gently, I felt a presence. The voice felt comforting, soothing, and very familiar.

Fortunately, I had encountered this voice a few times now and I immediately knew that it was God. Like a father speaking to his loving child, he began what I call his "God Whisper." Like twice before, he spoke telepathically. I understood everything he said, and I in return spoke to him telepathically. Immediately, I was witnessing a Cinemascope like vision of me talking to Sam earlier in the day. It was as if the replay button had been hit and I was an outside observer watching Sam and I engaged in the conversation we had experienced earlier. I watched Sam tell me again that he didn't believe in miracles and watched me tell him to just wait until the end of the week. As that vision diminished, I heard God's voice beckoning me to his urgent words, "People like Sam do not recognize that I perform miracles for them every day, both big and small. These miracles and signs are my kisses to them to let them know that I love them and am there for them. They think miracles have to be huge like the parting of the Red Sea, Jericho, Daniel, Lazarus. No, no! I perform miracles all the time!" Suddenly, in a flash, I saw the outline of a book. God began, like a magnificent artist painting on a canvas, directing, if you will, the contents of each half of a book. Pointing to the left side of the book, he said, "Tell them what miracles are and how they are to recognize them. Collect miracles from everyday people, telling their stories so that their stories can become testimonies of how much I love them."

He waved his right hand over the second part of the book. His voice was like a teacher's explaining a lesson to a student. "I want them to keep a journal of their miracles so they can look back at them and gain inspiration when they feel lonely and know that I was there with them every step of the way." He gave me specific directions for the journal, which I will reveal in a later chapter. He then whispered softly two times, **"Spirit within. Spirit within."** Telepathically, I somehow knew that God had given me the title of the book, but my humanness invoked me to ask him what *Spirit Within* had to do with miracles. I inquired, "Lord, do you want me to put a subtitle about miracles?" God lovingly whispered, "Remember the Trinity: the Father, Son, and Holy Spirit." His voice trailed off and I fell back into a deep slumber until my alarm went off. I didn't have a lot of time before breakfast, so I quickly scribbled the conversation as best as I could remember it. Usually when I am at home I keep a pad by my bed, and when I have these "God Whispers" I either write something down quickly on the pad or run downstairs to write it down before I forgot. Who would think that God would intervene during my vacation in Paris? Oh, he does have a sense of humor though. As quickly as I could get dressed, I found my new friends and could hardly contain myself, telling them about my revelation. They didn't act startled by my story at all but encouraged me to write the next book, but I argued that I had no intention of writing another book. They brought me back to reality by saying, "You're the one who believes in miracles. Now God has given you a mission. Are you going to do it or not?" Without hesitation, I replied, "Well, I guess I'm writing another book on miracles."

Later that day, they had someone come in and tell Christmas stories in the lounge. Denise and her mother decided to go, but I decided I'd better go back to the room and try to contact my family with my new tablet to let them know that I was safe. After I finally got the message sent and scribbled down the events in my journal with more details of the sights I had seen the previous day, I went to the lounge to find Denise and her mother. When I spotted Denise, her eyes were like a little child's opening Christmas presents. She was babbling about finding a pickle. I stopped her and said, "Slow down and tell me the whole story." Apparently, the storyteller told them a German classic fairytale about these children who were left alone and all they could find to eat were pickles. These pickles saved the children's lives and they lived happy ever after. (Personally, I would call this a miracle.) This story became a tradition and was told from one generation to another. To honor the classic fairytale, every Christmas a pickle is hidden in the Christmas tree. Whoever finds it receives a special gift. So Denise excitedly said, "Guess what? I found the pickle. Everyone was looking in the tree, but I decided to go ask the receptionist if it could be somewhere other than the tree." The receptionist told Denise, "I don't know!" Denise took that as a clue that perhaps it was somewhere else. She started looking all around the receptionist's desk, and to her surprise she found it inside a huge vase on the reception counter. Happily, she took the pickle to Sam, the program director, and received a set of Parisian stationery. At that moment, Sam interrupted because it was six thirty. We always met in the lounge so that Sam could give us a rundown of the next day's itinerary. Then as usual, he asked someone in the audience with pure hands to pull for a prize, one prize per night. All cabin numbers were placed in the basket. Someone from the audience volunteered and pulled the number. "Number 211," she called. Wow! That was Denise's cabin number. Denise shouted, "That's my number. I've won twice today!" She accepted the gift and looked at Sam. "Twice today, Sam!" He nodded in acknowledgement.

Sam continued by saying that they were going to have a big draw after dinner the next night and that the receptionist had tickets to sell for those who wanted to purchase them. Denise, her mom, and I left the lounge to go back to the room to change for dinner. About an hour later, I returned to the formal dining room and found Denise, her mom, and two more people sitting with them. Denise smiled, patted the chair next to her, and said, "We saved you a seat!" I said, "You all are so sweet. Thank you for thinking of me." The couple said, "Are you all traveling together?" We all blurted out that we just met at the airport and became instant friends. Everyone thought we had known each other all our lives. I considered it to be a miracle to find such generous, friendly people, because I was traveling alone. God had placed them in my life at just the right moment. Denise's voice jolted me back to reality. "Have you bought your tickets yet?"

"To what?" I asked. "The raffle tickets to the big draw after dinner tonight. I already bought three for ten euros and I'm going to win. I know I'm going to win. I already won twice. I just feel it," Laura exclaimed. Then she pointed to the couple and asked them if they were going to buy tickets and the man said no way was he going to waste money when Denise was so sure of herself. Well, that didn't stop me, because I believed in miracles, so I figured I at least had a chance. I excused myself and hurried off to purchase my three tickets. On the way back to the table, Denise was running past me, saying she was buying three more tickets for her mother. Boy, was she caught up in the excitement.

After dinner, we all went to the lounge. Laura joined us at the table and we all huddled with eager anticipation. Sam began by telling us that it was time for the draw and everyone needed to get their tickets out. As usual, he asked who had pure hands to draw the number. Laura's hands went up and she shouted, "Me!" Sam told her to come on up. She bounced up from her seat with joy. Sam's helper mixed up the numbers and just as Laura was putting her hands in the basket, Denise blurted, "Two-one-one." Out came Laura's hands and in disbelief, she screamed," Two-one-one." Sam's helper looked at the number again and said, "Yes, it is 211." Denise was in shock herself and went to collect her gift. She said to Sam, "Three prizes today!" Sam nodded. Denise was remembering what I had told her about Sam not believing in miracles. By that time, Denise was becoming a convert herself. When she returned to her seat, she asked me, "What's going on? This is weird. Am I psychic?" I said, "No, it's just your time." Two other numbers were called and then Laura pulled number 211 again! Denise was beside herself when she went up. She started apologizing to folks, saying the number was not hers but her mothers. When she returned to her seat, I saw her eyes tearing up. She was in a mesmerized state. I said, "We had better not win any more or these people are going to throw daggers at us. I'm not going to even think of my number." But the girl showing the prizes pulled out this huge jar of shower gel. It was the same one as the miniature they had in our rooms and I loved the silky feeling it gave you as the lather seemed to multiply all over the body. Without hesitation or thought, I blurted out, "I want that." I watched Laura pull out the number and blurt out in total disbelief, "Two-threethree," my room number. "Oh no!" I stammered. "I didn't mean to think it," I said to Denise. I stumbled up to get the gift and felt piercing eyes from the crowd. Denise and I were both in tears by then because we felt a supernatural presence. We just stared at each other, and then

I heard Laura's voice again, "Number 233." I felt faint; this couldn't be happening. I gathered myself together, and with my heart beating rapidly, I gained enough strength to get my gift. With tears in my eyes, I looked up at Sam. He threw up his hands as if to say, "I give up." I took that to mean he was caught up too in this supernatural moment. I found out later when I was more composed that I had won the DVD of all the spectacular places we were visiting on the ship. This was the DVD that everyone admired as it played daily on the receptionist desk. It was an absolute treasure.

After the draw, the captain came up to speak. He told everyone the unexpected news to the other passengers, "You are going to witness something that we have never had on this ship before in a few minutes." And suddenly the music began and Katlyn and Sal came strolling down the aisle with Katlyn looking beautiful with a white retro outfit and veil and Sal in his dapper black suit. To make this even more special, Laura performed the ceremony. Passengers were shocked but pleasantly surprised—another miracle for everyone. The wedding was so special.

The next morning, as I was going to breakfast I saw Sam. I looked at him and he looked at me. I said, "Now, Sam, do you believe in miracles?" Sam said, "A little bit more." That's all God needs, a crack in a doubter's heart, because then there's room for so many other miracles to fill his heart.

The night before we were to leave Paris, I spotted Laura in the reading section. She had been feeling very ill one of the days and we were all quite concerned. I went over to check on her. When she saw me, she grabbed both my hands. She said God had given her a revelation that everything was going to be all right. She said before she was worried about dying and rather scared but she was not afraid anymore. God had given her peace with whatever was to happen with her. Because we were in a public place she said, "Can you say a silent prayer with me?" And we did, with our eyes closed and heads bowed. At that very moment, God spoke to me, and I said, "Come with me to my cabin. I have something to give you." We entered my room and I reached for the bag of souvenirs I had bought to take home. Without hesitation, I unwrapped this beautiful white angel that I had bought for myself because I collect angels, and I gave it to her. She said, "No, I cannot accept it because you bought it for yourself." "I thought I was buying it for myself, but when we prayed together God whispered to me to give it to you as a gift from him. He wants you to know that he is with you and will take care of you." We hugged, not knowing if we would ever see each other again but knowing that God had put us in each other's lives for a reason. **As 2 Corinthians 13:14 says, "May the grace of the Lord Jesus, and the love of God, and the fellowship of the Holy Spirit be with you all."**

CHAPTER 15

MIRACLE STORIES TOLD TO ME

These miracle stories are written from friends, family and fellow Christians who honored God by testifying to the true miracles of his grace in their lives. The stories are breathtaking, courageous, inspirational, shockingly honest and utterly engaging as they recap events in their lives that without the presence of the Holy Spirit could have tumbled them into a world of despair. By their courage in telling these stories, others will gain confidence knowing that their circumstance can also turn into a positive if they just believe and trust in the power of God's goodness. Once you put your life in God's hands and turn your troubles over to him, you will develop a relationship like no other and your life will never be the same. The miracles that occurred in the lives of the writers will live on to inspire and enrich the lives of others. **The book Matthew 28:19 says, "Therefore go and make disciples of all nations...."**

Miracle A

*Miracles by M. P.,
East Bay*

These three stories happened to me several years ago. This was during a period of time in my life where I was searching for God with my whole being, heart, soul, and body. I was praying many hours a day, seeking the Lord in prayer, praying to the Holy Spirit, Bible study, starting a Bible club for the students of Bishop School, and attending many church gatherings of believers. During my daily tasks during this time of my life, I was in deep intercession for strangers standing in lines, walking down sidewalks, and prayed almost constantly in my daily activities. This period of my life was an intense God period, unlike any other in my walk except for the first "honeymoon" period when I had just heard the Good News and had accepted Christ as my savior while in college many years prior.

I cannot really explain why this period of time occurred in my life, as my life has now returned to a much more normal pace. All I know is that I saw miracles happen to people I knew and to myself during this time. The three that I care to share are just the most dramatic and most notable, but this is not meant to negate the other God moments I had during this period of time.

Miracle no. 1: The wedding ring

This happened on Easter morning several years ago. I woke up early, like I do often, and had a deep desire to spend some quiet time with Jesus before church. I went on about a 2½ mile walk in my neighborhood, where I have been known to walk a common established route. And throughout the walk I was praying and singing and listening to gospel music, and completely happy, knowing I was close to God. I came home and got ready for church the normal way and did not notice until my hands were raised over my head in the middle of the church service that the 1.2-carat diamond in my wedding ring had disappeared! I was rather shocked, but just continued through the church service without saying anything except to my husband. I just prayed that God would help me find it! I told my friends at church to look on the carpet and let me know if they found anything.

After I got home, I was bummed; therefore, I decided to retrace my steps all the way back through the miles that I had walked, praying and walking while searching, to no avail. I went on with the Easter day as normal with my family, cooking and washing dishes and every so often looking all over the carpet floors of my house, hoping by some chance the diamond would appear. When I went to bed that night, just before I went to sleep I confessed to God that this diamond ring being lost was ruining my peace and destroying my fellowship with him, and I confessed that it was taking up way too much of my attention. And then I just gave it to him to deal with. I was done. After all, it was just a ring, it was not as important as my dear husband, and certainly not worth getting all upset about. I said I could be happy with a fake cubic zirconium if need be, and went to sleep to forget about it.

The next morning was a school day, and as usual I needed to race to get ready and out the door on time. I said hi to the Lord as I woke up, and as soon as I realized I was awake, I felt a huge desire to go check the carpet right by my dresser. It was as if I

woke up and was driven by a motor to go check this one part of my room. The diamond was right on the carpet, where I always got dressed. I yelled to my husband, "I found it!" Neither he nor I have ever been able to figure why we never saw it there before. I have always wondered if an angel returned it in the middle of the night.

Miracle no. 2: The coffee cup

This happened in my classroom in Room 14 at Bishop Elementary School. It happened right after, maybe a few months after, the diamond-reappearing miracle. It was morning, maybe 9:00 AM.

It was just a few days after a major vacation break, and I was really sleepy and feeling unenergetic that day. It was on a Monday, because I had Bible club that afternoon and I would be the teacher. I needed all the pep I could get!

I decided to make myself a cup of instant coffee, so I put the hot water heater on, which was in a corner of classroom, and went back to teaching. When the water came to a boil, I picked up my coffee cup and realized it was not completely clean. So I poured some of the boiling hot water in it, all the way to the top, and some liquid soap so that it would get sparkly clean. Just then, one of my students came up and asked me a quick question, and because I was in a hurry to get back to teaching, I mistakenly put my hand into the cup to wash it out. I had my hand in boiling hot water! Many years ago, I had a finger accident and I have to wear my wedding ring on my right hand. So my right hand was completely hot, and I put it immediately in cold water at the sink. I immediately realized the danger I had created for myself, and under my breath I said a quick prayer, "Please, Jesus, help me! Don't let this be a bad burn!"

After I said that prayer, I immediately went back to teaching without even thinking about my hand. My students needed me and my attention and I was no longer sleepy! I never did drink that cup of coffee!

I taught the rest of the day and all through Bible club, and went home normally that night like nothing out of the usual had happened that day! I literally forgot about it. It was completely erased from my mind! I did not even tell my husband. It was as if it had never happened. My hand was completely normal; there was absolutely no sign whatsoever of any burn.

The next morning, as usual, I got up early to go swimming before school, and I always take off my wedding ring and set it on top of the microwave until I got home. I just don't like to swim with it on in case something might happen to it in the pool.

My husband greeted me at the door after I came home from my swim, as he had noticed that my ring looked weird. He asked me, "What the heck did you do yesterday that would cause your ring to look like this?"

I was embarrassed to tell him, but did tell him what happened the day before. Both he and I were aware at that moment that a miracle had occurred. My ring was completely out of shape; it was no longer round. It had molded itself to the shape of my finger, and it was completely distorted and bent out of shape. It looked as if someone had taken the metal and just banged it hard to reshape it to a weird, distorted shape. It was completely deformed, but still intact. The diamond itself was the same.

I took the ring to my favorite jeweler, the one who had heard the ring miracle no. 1 and fixed it that time.

Now I was back with another miracle story. When I told him, he said that the gold had melted to the shape of my finger and that could only happened at extremely high temperatures, and that I should have been in the emergency room immediately after that happened. He testified that another miracle had happened to my ring; that could be the only explanation in his professional experience.

Praise God! I should have been disfigured, but instead he supernaturally intervened and healed my hand!

Miracle no. 3: The jewelry box

This was a dream. I dreamed that I was in a glorious room that was filled from floor to ceiling with extravagantly decorated jewelry boxes. The entire room was so brilliant that your eyes could barely stand the reflection of the light. The boxes ranged in sizes, but all were completely covered in radiant diamonds. I felt as if I was in the jewelry storeroom of heaven.

I bent down to see one of the jewelry boxes and I realized that the boxes had tickets on them. One part of the ticket said "Admit One" and the other part had a name on it. I asked what the names meant, and the Lord told me that these were his children, his jewels.

I woke up realizing that some of those names were the names of students I had once taught!

The Lord, I feel, was telling me how happy he was with the Bishop Bible Club!

By Mary Pound

Miracle B

My Miracle Baby
by S. P., Northern California

My husband and I dreamed of having a beautiful baby girl and fortunately we found out that I was indeed expecting a girl. We went to the doctor and even heard the song "Isn't She lovely" by Stevie Wonder and were convinced this was a sign from God. Needless to say, we were ecstatic.

At twenty-four weeks' gestation, I began feeling some pains. I was leading a school through its accreditation process and was in the middle of the meeting when all of a sudden I began profusely bleeding. I began shaking, went downstairs, and the school secretary rushed me to the hospital. When I was checked, the doctor told me that I was losing the baby and placed a pan under me "just in case." I was devastated. My husband rushed to the hospital and we were utterly heartbroken as doctors came in and said that we would have to sign papers to keep the baby alive even if she were to have severe deformities, neurological damage, and other defects. We obviously signed, and just prayed and prayed. They kept taking us to the sonography room, and at that time, a nurse whispered to me that I would be okay and held my hand, saying she was a laysister of Mother Theresa's order and that she was praying, that I would be well, and with a healthy baby. I held her hand and was scared out of my mind. The only person to comfort me was that unnamed, unknown, mysterious nurse.

The next day, my father visited me at the hospital because my husband was at work. He sat in my hospital room as I lay in bed and began talking about his mother, my paternal grandmother who was a survivor of the Armenian genocide and happened to be a nurse/midwife. I have always considered her an inspiration, one who has survived in the face of adversity, and we began to talk about "what she would have said" and "how she would have lightened up the mood" if she saw what was happening. Right when we were having that discussion, a nurse knocked on my door and said, "Hello, I want to talk to you as a friend of the Armenians." We were shocked and welcomed her, asking her how she knew I was Armenian, and it was through seeing my last name, which like all Armenians', ends in *-ian*. She then closed the door and said, "I am a midwife, and I want to tell you how to get through this and get better. You are to eat dried apricots, which are hematocrit makers, and visualize positive things happening to your body. Rest assured, you are going to be fine, and your daughter will be safe and you will not go into labor this early." My father and I were shocked. We felt my grandmother's presence; God's presence was there and he sent these angels to protect me and my family. The next day, another doctor came in and told me that I was okay, that my situation had stabilized, and although I was better, I was to stay in bed rest for the remainder of my pregnancy. My daughter was born at almost thirty-five weeks, almost ten weeks later. And although she was premature, she was perfect and healthy, and to this day remains a positive, healthy, miracle child. We named her "Areni," which in Armenian means "gift from heaven." She is indeed a gift from God, as all babies are. And ten years later, we are enjoying all of her miracles.

Every day I thank God for his angels, who guide me through every trial and tribulation. Whether it is for my daughter's continued health or the little miracles he places in my path, or for the guidance of the angels that are always around me.

Miracle C

In Loving Memory of My Son by S. S., Northern California

Psalm 34:18

The Lord is close to the brokenhearted and saves those who are crushed in spirit.

And thus the story of simply one of my many miraculous gifts from my Lord, the Almighty.

The horrible phone call that changed my life forever arrived in the wee hours of the morning on December 9, 2002. Slumber had always come easily for me, a time to rest my soul and quiet the mind. I was deeply sound asleep. The words resonated like a lingering knife piercing my heart: a horrible accident... severely injured by a drunk driver. What came out of my mouth was foreign; the wail was long and animalistic. Within twelve hours, my only child, Jason, was pronounced brain dead at the age of twenty-seven. His partner, Kristin, was one-month pregnant. My heart was shredded, broken, collapsed, and weeping. My soul was covered in desolation. I was left with the "essence" of my son, a broken person.

The birth of my granddaughter was incontestably bittersweet; however, I fell in love immediately. She was born on a sunny and warm August day, with a noticeable gentle breeze. The perfect setting for a new birth. Alexandra Jace's baptism was set for two months later in a Catholic church in Indiana (where Kristin had gone to be with her parents). The trip for the baptism was marked by sadness, as seemingly the whole year was. My husband, who was chosen to be the godfather, could not attend due to mitigating circumstances at work. I, the chosen godmother, was solo in my flight and seemingly in my thoughts. I brought Jason's baptismal candle, several framed photos of him and my broken heart. He would witness the baptism, if only in pictures. I so wanted him there. Arriving in Indiana the night before gave Kristin, her mother, and I time to grieve together. Kristin's parents had divorced, so the sacred event was to be witnessed by only us three women and one two-month-old child. This seemed to add to the disparity of the event and clouded with shrouds what should have been a joyous occasion—to witness a child blessed into the life of Christianity. Tears were readily falling on our way to St. Joseph's Church that Sunday morning and we couldn't stop. The mass was further interrupted with the sound of shrill cries coming from baby Alexandra. Kristin forgot the bottle and Alexandra's perception of "quiet" at mass was not yet instilled. After mass, Fr. Bernie solemnly walked toward us and informed us he needed to have a private conversation. Apparently, there were two families baptizing children that day. One that had ceremoniously brought their extended families and had a gathering of over thirty people, and us. Would we mind if he were to baptize Alexandra first, as the second baptism would most likely be lengthy? With Alexandra's stomach still churning for food, we gladly agreed. I walked to the altar, placed Jason's beautifully framed picture, lit his baptismal candle, and cried. The tears were coming so fast I didn't bother to wipe them away. At that point, Fr. Bernie asked, albeit politely, where the godfather was? We explained to him that my husband was not able to attend, as much as he wanted to be there. Of course this brought more weeping and sadness. Fr. Bernie continued to explain that we would need a male figure to witness the baptism in my husband's place, and that my husband would still be listed as the godfather. We froze. Neither Kristin nor her mother knew anyone else in the small town, much less a male. Once again I began to cry, holding the picture of Jason tightly against my heart and wondering if life could possibly get worse. At that moment Fr. Bernie asked if it would be okay if he asked someone from the other baptismal group if they were willing to stand in as a witness. Moments later he returned with a handsome young man who looked to be in his mid-twenties. The entire experience thus far seemed surreal, which seemed to mimic my pervasive existence. At the moment the young man walked over all I could think was why can't my son be here? I extended my hand to shake the young man's extended hand as he said, "Hello, my name is Jason." I looked at Kristin, whose knees were buckling, grabbed her arm to steady her, felt a peaceful, warm glow take over my entire body, and knew without a doubt that I had just experienced a miracle. The miraculous, infinite glory of God!

— Sandra Pertile Summers,
in honor of my son, Jason Christopher Pertile

Miracle D

Hawaii's Road to Hana by C. D., East Bay

Every summer my wife and I plan a family trip together with my two daughters. This year was no exception, and we were all especially excited because we were going to beautiful Maui, Hawaii. As usual, I had mapped out some fun and intriguing tours for our days there.

On this particular day, we were going to visit the famous Road to Hana. Maui wouldn't be complete without a tour to this magnificent place, we were told. The Road to Hana was an all-day trip filled with God's handiwork. Some say the sights were as close to Heaven as one could get. The towering waterfalls were majestic and stunning, and the lush green landscape was spectacular. Clear, sparkling beaches surrounded curving mountainsides. This truly was amazing.

So there we were, driving along the beautiful landscape in our rented convertible Mustang without a care in the world. It started sprinkling a little on the way as is known to happen in that part of the country, so I put the top up for a while. The roads were winding with blind turns, high cliffs, and one-lane roads over bridges, but we didn't care because we were having a great time. The girls were sitting in the back, chatting back and forth with me and their mom about the lovely sights. The sun was still gleaming down upon us and pretty soon the girls started asking if I could let the top back down because the rain had stopped. I let it down to get some fresh air in for a while. We all got out a couple of times to view some sacred sights and other scenery. After visiting and taking a dip in the pools of Ohe'o (a.k.a. Seven Sacred Pools), we decided it was getting late and started to make our way back to the resort.

As we were headed back, something kept telling me to put the top up. I thought it was rather odd because it wasn't raining. However, the voice in my head was persistent. As I began to put the top up, the girls were yelling for me to keep it down, but I persisted on rolling up the top. Halfway back to the resort, with the girls sulking in the backseat, we heard a large thud on the top of the car, right above where the girls were seated. The girls were frightened as the loud sound startled all of us. We all looked around, wondering what in the heck had landed on the top of the car, but it was too difficult to pull over on the winding road. Hastily, we headed back to the hotel and got out to inspect the car. To our surprise, there was a big dent exactly where one of my daughters was sitting. One of the Hawaiians said it was probably a coconut because it was more common than people think that some people who sit under coconut trees die of head injuries from falling coconuts. Wow! We all thought how lucky we were. As years passed and I became more in tune with God's grace and miracles, I realized that God's voice was what I had heard telling me to close the top on the car. Now, when I hear that voice in my head, listen. God doesn't steer us wrong.

The miracle stories you have read hopefully will inspire you and encourage you to look for the everyday miracles which occur on a daily basis. Believe in miracles and God's blessings and your life will reap the benefits of a spiritual awakening like never before. I hope you enjoy this poem below. I certainly believe in miracles because I am one.

MIRACLE, I AM

Angels are always looking after me!

I know I am a miracle
For God has blessed me so
He saved me from surgeries and illnesses
Which left me at an all-time low.

I wonder how some people cope
When their entire world collapse
Without the love of God and hope
They fall into unavoidable traps

Faith keeps me going from day to day
Knowing my God is by my side
I know that HE will lead the way
For my health and well- being cannot hide.

Author-Frances Purnell-Dampier

www.ingramcontent.com/pod-product-compliance
Lightning Source LLC
LaVergne TN
LVHW051954060526
838201LV00059B/3643